BEHIND the BIGLAW CURTAIN

Demystifying the Junior Associate Experience: How to Succeed as a Junior Lawyer in Biglaw

MARISSA GEANNETTE

Marissa Geannette
The Unbillable Life Press
For more information and resources,
visit www.behindthebiglawcurtain.com and
www.theunbillablelife.com
or reach out to marissa@theunbillablelife.com.

Printed in the United States of America
First Printing 2020
First Edition 2020

ISBN: 978-1-7349223-1-8

To my fellow class of 2008 summer associates, who fumbled through Biglaw with me from the very beginning. Without you guys (and all of our lunches, coffee breaks, and happy hours at the Long Room and the Pig & Whistle), I would never have survived working in Biglaw for as long (or as happily) as I did.

Table of Contents

Preface

A Peek Behind the Curtain

What Is Biglaw?

Before we really get into it, we must clearly set the stage and define *Biglaw*, the backdrop for every story and piece of advice in this book. Biglaw is the term given to the behemoth law firms of the world that are mostly headquartered in New York City and have offices spanning the globe. You will find Biglaw firms in all major cities and many, many smaller ones.

At the end of their first year of law school, eager young law students are recruited to work at these firms for ten or twelve weeks the following summer (after their second year of law school). Then, if everything works out, after graduating from law school, they begin their careers as associates at the same firm they worked at the prior summer. They work long and hard and eventually (hopefully? possibly?) become law firm partners eight or ten years later.

Hold up – not so fast. That was the traditional path, but times have changed. Most people who enter Biglaw as associates won't stay long enough to make partner, either because they aren't cut out for the job or because they don't want a Biglaw career and the lifestyle that comes with it.

Biglaw firms handle the most complex transactions in the world, from mergers of giant public companies, to initial public offerings of foreign companies into the U.S. market, to litigations where billions of dollars are at stake. The stakes are high and the work is demanding. The rewards for working in Biglaw include the chance to work with brilliant people on high-profile deals and, let's not forget to mention, lots of money. For all of this, however, there is a trade-off. "Work-life balance" in the world of Biglaw is not exactly balanced.

To succeed in Biglaw, it takes more than a stellar academic record and it takes more than dedication and hard work, which is where this book comes in. There are so many things you need to know about Biglaw that aren't taught in law school, that you won't find in any career books, and, frankly, that have nothing to do with the law. Biglaw can be a mystifying place for junior associates. They are thrown in and expected to know the rules without ever being told them. You can learn on the fly, making mistakes as you go, or you can get a head start and learn what you need to know here first. It's up to you.

I've pulled back the curtain on Biglaw to offer you an insider's look into what goes on behind the scenes. It's all about business, though. You won't find any salacious stories here (you can find those on legal blogs such as *Above the Law*), but there will be plenty of inside knowledge and tips on how to succeed as a junior associate in a pressure cooker of a legal world.

Who Is This Book For?

This book is for anyone who is thinking about entering, is about to begin work in, or is already embedded in the crazy world that is Biglaw. It is for the law student attending on-campus interviews (known as "OCI") who is wondering what lies behind the glossy sheen of the firms she is visiting.

It is for the first-year associate who feels like he is spending his entire life at his firm and yet is somehow still screwing everything up.

While this book is tailored to specific situations that happen in Biglaw offices around the world, much of the advice holds true for many legal jobs. Whether you are a corporate, non-profit, or government attorney, much of what Biglaw demands of its associates, such as producing impeccable work product, is valuable at any of these jobs. Hopefully, though, those of you not in Biglaw can skip over the Biglaw-specific topics, like the importance of billing your time (every second counts) and planning a vacation (in Biglaw, there's an art to this).

Lastly, this book is for those of you who are merely interested in what the heck goes on at a place where a person who just graduated from law school and has no prior work experience gets paid almost $200,000 a year. Given the opportunity, would you put up with Biglaw for that amount of money? Most people would say yes, and I said yes, too, for almost eight years.

If I had known from the outset how to better navigate the topics and situations I have written about here, my time in Biglaw would have gone a lot smoother. However, that does not mean that I would still be in Biglaw. In fact, my time there would have been shorter, if anything, had I known all that I know now. That is because this book is not just about navigating some of the tricky issues that arise for most junior associates. It is also about putting the time into planning your career, instead of letting it take you along for the ride, because if you allow it to, Biglaw will do just that. Becoming a successful Biglaw associate is not just about surviving the first few years of Biglaw. While I'll help you to do that, I also want to show you that you have control over your Biglaw career, even if it doesn't always feel like that.

So whoever you are, whether you are an enthusiastic first-year associate striving to be perfect at everything you do (hint: that's impossible in Biglaw) or are just curious about what goes on at a Biglaw firm, this book is for you. Enjoy it, and, hopefully, my advice resonates with you and saves you from committing a faux pas, getting lost in the shuffle, working with the wrong people, or staying at a job you dislike for years or even just one day too long.

I hope this book fills in the gaps and teaches you the things your firm doesn't teach you, but should, and those that, without this book, you would only be able to learn after being on the ground in Biglaw for years. Combine the tips you'll take away from this book with the substantive legal skills you'll develop on the job, and I'm sure you'll become an excellent attorney and an all-star Biglaw associate.

Why Am I Qualified to Write This Book?

Biglaw is unlike any other workplace, and I spent eight years of my life entrenched in it, first as a summer associate and then as an associate in the New York City office of a top twenty international law firm. Aside from my first year at work, when I received assignments from several corporate groups, I was a member of the Capital Markets Group during my tenure at the firm. I practiced in a very specific area of the law, but I gained a broad experience.

Not only did I work on deals across the firm with associates and partners from other offices and other groups, such as intellectual property, tax, employee benefits, and even litigation once in a while, I also worked on various firm committees with people from all practice areas and all departments. During my time in Biglaw, I worked with some of the most brilliant lawyers around.

When it came to that critical time in my career, the transition from senior associate to potentially making partner (definitely not a guaranteed bridge you will get to, let alone cross), I took a step back and assessed my career and life. I faced a mini-crisis because I had known deep-down for a long time that Biglaw was not where I wanted to be and not what I wanted to do. I knew that I probably should have left a couple of years before I did, but I stayed. In this book, I advise against doing what I did: putting your head in the sand until you wake up one day and realize, you've reached the point of burnout.

Even though I ultimately decided that a long-term career in Biglaw was not for me, I still put in the work for eight years. That puts me in the somewhat unique position of having completed the whole associate track, from junior to mid-level to senior, so I know what it's like to work at every level.

Aside from the time I spent in Biglaw, I have something else valuable to share with you that many in Biglaw do not: I am empathetic and highly perceptive of the world around me. I know how to read what the room needs and I can adapt to those needs. As you advance in your career and the years go by, you naturally start to forget what it was like for you in the beginning. The gap between the junior associates and the more senior associates and partners widens. Even the mid-levels start to forget that they, too, used to make the same mistakes, not that long ago, that the juniors are making today.

Being empathetic and perceptive meant that I could still relate to the junior associates when I was an eighth-year associate. I had not forgotten what a struggle it was to be a junior associate, and I know that this made me a better colleague and mentor to those more junior to me. In this book, I aim to provide you with that same empathetic viewpoint and those same mentorship skills.

What Makes This Book Different From the Others?

There are a couple of other books out there written for Biglaw associates. I remember devouring them when I was starting out in my career, looking for any nugget of advice that would serve me in the years to come. While I did find some things helpful, there wasn't one book that gave me everything I was after.

Unlike some of the others, this book isn't written just for those who want to make partner. I know from experience that not only is partnership *not* the goal of most junior associates, but it is not realistic for most, either. Most associates enter Biglaw hoping to pay off student loans, receive excellent legal training, and learn valuable skills that they can take to any future job. They don't enter Biglaw looking ahead ten years to the corner office. For that reason, this book teaches you how to be the best junior associate you can be, no matter what your end goal is.

This book is also filled with real-life examples, not lofty, abstract goals that you can't reach. What's the point in telling a junior associate that he should get to the office early every day, work diligently and uninterrupted until 7:00 p.m., take a few moments at the end of his workday to write out the next day's to-do list, and leave the office at 7:30 p.m., when Biglaw's reality is far from that? I tell you how things actually work and how you can succeed within the parameters of Biglaw's reality.

What This Book Is Not

I want to be clear about what this book is not. This book isn't going to teach you the substantive skills you need to master to succeed at Biglaw. There would be almost no point in going through the detailed work that a junior associate will encounter (document review, due diligence review, coordinating closings, drafting interrogatories, drafting officers' certificates, forming corporations; the list is endless) because the skills an associate in one group needs to master are wildly different from the skills an associate in another group will need to know.

Whenever I would sit at lunch with my friends in the litigation group and listen to them talk about their work (writing briefs, analyzing expert reports, preparing witnesses), it was as if they were speaking another language. I truly had no idea what they did all day, and they felt the same way about me and my work. Even working with one partner versus another in the same group will vary greatly. It will vary from corporate group to corporate group, between corporate and litigation, and from firm to firm. What you learn on one deal, one project, or one case won't directly translate to the next deal, project, case, or job.

However, the general skills you will gain in Biglaw *will* be transferable to almost anything you do. For this reason, I give more general (yet specific to Biglaw) advice in this book. It will become clear as you read on that while this book is aimed at specific situations that you will encounter in Biglaw, you will gain an abundance of knowledge that is relevant no matter what practice group you are in, what law firm you are at, and what job you end up at, if one day you decide to leave Biglaw.

Even though this book is not focused on substantive legal skills, mastering those skills and becoming an excellent attorney is, without a doubt, the number one most crucial piece of the puzzle that makes up a successful Biglaw career. I trust that you will acquire those legal skills on the job by working as hard as you can, dedicating yourself to your firm, and learning from the best and the brightest.

This book is also not going to directly teach you how to get clients or build a book of business. I did, however, want to acknowledge that this is an important skill to develop during your associate years, as having a book of business is necessary to succeed as a Biglaw partner. If partnership is on your mind, there are some great resources out there that can help you get started on building relationships with clients and even getting some of your own as an associate, as it is never too early to start that process. You should, however, use the skills you'll learn in this book to become the best lawyer you can be so that when you are put in front of a client and are given a chance to show off your skills, you'll impress them so much they'll be begging to hire you.

Oh, and this book isn't going to tell you what to wear to work. By now, you all know how to look professional and put together (if you don't, look it up online before your first day in Biglaw). Turns out, fashion doesn't matter in Biglaw, but your work ethic, how you interact with clients, your ability to juggle multiple tasks at once, and much more, all do, so that's what we're going to focus on here.

Why Did I Write This Book?

Lastly, I want to let you know why I wrote this book. As I mentioned at the beginning of this *Preface*, I want to demystify the world of Biglaw for those who are intimidated, scared, or nervous to work there. I want to pull back the curtain to show you that it's not so scary after all, so long as you learn the rules and play by them. What's another way of expressing pulling back the curtain? Well, Biglaw, of course, taught me its own way of saying this. Let me explain.

Working in Biglaw, and in the business world in general, will expose you to unfamiliar terms and phrases. One such phrase I learned on the job that I found to be both amusing and slightly horrifying was "open the kimono." The term means that all of the details about a situation will be shared with everyone involved and no information will be held back.

The first time I heard this phrase was during a conference call with a client, a public company going through some major problems. Various parties were on the line to brainstorm a possible solution to a dire situation. To set a tone of transparency, the general counsel of the company began the call by stating that he was going to "open the kimono" on the situation. For the next five minutes, I suppressed laughter and tried to regain my focus. It was difficult to recover from the thought of the general counsel of a public company wearing only a brightly colored kimono and opening that kimono to periodically flash the room while we seriously discussed the details of a complex transaction.

While this is not a pretty image, it is one that I could joke about with the other associate in the room at the time, who happens to be one of my best friends to this day. As serious as the work in Biglaw is, there are also moments of levity. Even with all of the crazy people you will come across, you will make some genuinely great friends at the firm, too.

In honor of everything that Biglaw is: demanding, rewarding, challenging, fast-paced, tough, entertaining, a place where real friendships are formed, and so much more, I am going to pull back the curtain and "open the kimono" on the world of Biglaw. These are my insider tips and advice on how to succeed as a junior associate. My goal is for this book to be the resource for you that I wish I'd had as a junior associate, so you don't have to struggle through those early years like I did.

Introduction

The Three Key Qualities That Make a Junior Associate Useful

Notice that this *Introduction* isn't titled "Qualities That Make a Junior Associate *Exceptional*" or "*Outstanding*." Instead, I said *useful*. To achieve the accolades of exceptional or outstanding, associates must do much more than display the following three qualities. However, cultivating these is a great place to start.

If you don't have the time to read anything else in this book, at least read these next few pages before you begin your Biglaw career. As with much of the advice in this book, these qualities don't have anything to do with your legal knowledge. Even if you lack confidence in your legal skills, you can start your career on the right foot by displaying these three qualities from day one.

1. Ownership

The first must-have quality is what many in the Biglaw world call "ownership," and it boils down to taking responsibility for and pride in your work. Translated to the Biglaw world, this means that for every single task you are assigned, no matter how insignificant or complicated it may be, treat the assignment with the care and attention you would a high-stakes matter.

"Owning it" can be challenging at times. For one, some of the tasks assigned to junior associates could be completed by fifth-graders. When working on one of these assignments, I often thought that I could have bribed a hardworking ten-year-old with some ice cream and she would have been very useful in taking the task off of my plate. It doesn't matter that a task might be "beneath" your education level. Take ownership and make sure there's not one thing out of place when you turn the assignment in. Only by taking ownership of the more trivial aspects of the job will you be "awarded" with more substantive (and usually more interesting) work, so taking ownership is to your long-term advantage.

Other times, you will receive a task that is so above your head no matter how many questions you ask or how hard you work on it, that your work product will be far from perfect. In these situations, taking ownership of your work is just as, if not more, important. Always make sure that whatever you turn in is as good as it can be, given your abilities. Presentation goes a long way. Ownership, in some cases, might just mean that you've formatted a document correctly, printed it out, highlighted relevant sections, and given it to the senior associate to further review.

Hold yourself accountable for all of the tasks you are given, no matter who "below" or "above" you in the Biglaw hierarchy you are working with (more on the importance of the Biglaw hierarchy in *Chapter One*). Is an email addressed to you? Own it and respond. Did you make a mistake (more on that later, too)? Own it and fix it. Ultimately, it's about being responsible for the work you produce and the mistakes you make.

2. Availability

A second and equally important quality is your availability to work: at all times. You may think that being available 99% of the time is good enough, but it's not. If someone tries to contact you during the 1% of the time when you're not answering your phone or emails, or you've stepped out of the office early, you risk having your one-time unresponsiveness forever brand you as unreliable.

Fortunately, being "available" all of the time does not mean that you actually have to be available to work 24/7. In practice, it means that you must be ready and willing to work all of the time, unless you have clearly communicated with your team exactly when you will *not* be available.

As a junior associate, the time you are allowed to be unavailable (without someone more senior thinking that you don't take your job seriously) is pretty limited. You are expected to be able to work whenever something comes in the door, whether that is during business hours, at 2:00 a.m., or over the weekend. Luckily, as you get further along in your career, you'll be better able to anticipate when the work will come in, but in the beginning, you usually won't be privy to that information.

Technology allows you to be available almost all of the time, no matter where you are, which is both a good thing and a bad thing. It allows you to leave the office when you are waiting for a document to come across from the other side so you can go about your life, instead of sitting at your desk for three hours waiting. But it also allows you to work remotely and during non-business hours, such as all weekend or while on vacation. Striking a balance between work and the rest of your life (which we discuss in

Chapters Nineteen and *Twenty*, and which is one of the hardest parts of Biglaw to master) is a crucial skill to learn early on.

3. Enthusiasm

Lastly, useful Biglaw associates who are on their way to becoming excellent ones are always enthusiastic. You've just been told that the team is staying late tonight (again) to finish up an offering document? Your response: sounds good, what can I do to help? Nobody has volunteered to draft a client alert that is due in ten hours? Your response: you raise your hand, volunteer, and start writing.

It will be hard to show enthusiasm sometimes, like when you are exhausted or when you are not interested in a particular assignment, but you can and should remain engaged and enthusiastic. If a senior attorney takes the time to explain the nuances of a transaction to you, even if that explanation is way over your head or is boring you to tears, act interested. Feign enthusiasm if you have to.

You can show enthusiasm by asking questions and engaging in the materials. For example, if a partner in your group shares an article about the newest market trends in your industry, even if you don't expect to work on that type of deal, read the article and ask the partner a question about it. This isn't kissing up, even if it sounds like it. It's learning how to play the Biglaw game. The good thing is that, as a junior associate, it's almost always easy to be enthusiastic. If you arrive at a meeting with a smile, a notebook, and the relevant documents, that's a great start.

~ ~ ~

A junior associate who takes ownership of her work, is available whenever needed, and is enthusiastic no matter what the circumstances are, will be useful to senior attorneys and clients. Now that we've gotten those basics out of the way, let's dive into how you can become not just a useful junior associate, but an exceptional and outstanding one.

Chapter One

The Biglaw Hierarchy

You know the Beyoncé song "Irreplaceable"? She might as well be singing about Biglaw junior associates when she says, "I can have another you by tomorrow; so don't you ever for a second get to thinking you're irreplaceable."

Most of us grew up being told how special we were (I am talking to you, fellow Millennials and Gen Z-ers) and this is true; you are unique and don't you forget it! However, in the eyes of Biglaw, one first-year associate is the same as any other one. You regain an identity as you become more senior and more entrenched on teams and with clients, but you have to put in the work and the time to make this happen.

This is not meant to discourage you, but rather to show you your place in the Biglaw hierarchy. When you arrive in Biglaw, you will have just gone through the courting process that is OCI. Multiple firms will have told you how much they want you to work at their firm and how amazing you are, but that is just part of the game.

All Biglaw firms compete for a relatively small pool of talent and they shower law students with praise to woo them to their firm. Once that talent (you) arrives at work, the slate is wiped clean. It does not matter where you went to law school or whether or not you were on law review, you sit at the bottom of the Biglaw food chain, and you and the associate in the next office over will be seen as interchangeable.

To set the stage for how this can play out, let me tell you about a deal I worked on as a first-year associate. I was staffed on an M&A deal that was so huge and had so many attorneys working on it that I never met the partners who were running the show. This staffing structure was not typical of my Biglaw experience, but it is how massive deals are often staffed. It was on this deal that I learned that I was replaceable and interchangeable with just about anyone.

On the morning of the deal's closing, everyone who had worked on the deal, partners included, sat in a giant conference room on the top floor of our office building, surrounded by folders upon folders of original documents. The partner was going to make a series of phone calls to the trustee to close the multiple transactions in a very particular order. Unbeknownst to me, since I'd never been a part of a closing like this before, he needed someone to record the exact time that each piece of the transaction had closed before we could move on to closing the next one.

By this point, I had been up for a few days and nights in a row and was relieved it was finally the morning of closing and I could just sit back and observe. That is, until the partner who I had never met began shouting, "Katie, are you writing this down? Katie? Katie?" I casually scanned the room and, realizing there was nobody there named Katie, nor anyone who could possibly be named Katie, figured out that he was talking to me. So I did what any good first-year associate does and I said, "Of course, I'm writing it all down," and I did. He did not care who Katie was, be it a paralegal, a first-year associate, or a robot, as long as the job he needed to get done got done.

The transaction closed and nobody ever asked me for those closing notes. I would see that partner occasionally over the next few years and would always smile to myself knowing that I survived that deal. I had recognized my place in the Biglaw hierarchy and dutifully played my part.

Now that you understand your place in the Biglaw hierarchy, how do you begin to set yourself apart from the other associates who you began your career being viewed as interchangeable with? Here are a few ways to provide value to those more senior members on your team, while transitioning yourself from replaceable to irreplaceable along the way.

Practical Ways to Provide Value to Those More Senior to You

Law firms are filled with intelligent, focused, motivated, determined, ambitious, and, to put it nicely, "quirky" people. Making partner in Biglaw requires a certain combination of factors to come together all at once. Legal acumen, good market timing, and a whole lot of hard work, energy, and devotion to the job are required. By the time someone has made partner, he has sacrificed so much and has spent an incredible number of hours getting deals done and cases won.

The result of all of this hard work and sacrifice is a partner who has developed a very particular way of getting things done, and getting things done well. And it's not just the partners who are particular. By the time someone is a few years into his career, he starts to develop a specific way he expects things to get done.

The following four pieces of advice will serve as your baseline for how to provide value to these partners and senior associates. By following these tips and going above and beyond what a "useful" associate described in the *Introduction* would do, people will be begging to have you on their team.

1. Be Adaptable

The primary job of a junior associate is to be of service to those more senior to him. In recognizing the quirks of those senior to you and adapting to them, you'll put yourself in the best position to be of service. As a junior associate, your initial clients are the senior attorneys you work with, the most important being the lead partner on the matter. It is, therefore, your job to make that partner's job easier. It is unlikely a partner will change her ways and adapt to *you* (nor should you expect her to), so it is your job as the associate to figure out what those ways are and how to work with them.

How can you do this? First, when staffed on a project with a new group of lawyers, take the time to figure out, either by asking the senior person directly or by asking another associate about her, how she likes things done. Even better, take it one step further and figure out how everyone senior to you, not just the partner, works and what their individual preferences are.

You can figure some of this out by asking the person directly when she gives you an assignment. Other times, it makes more sense to ask the group's paralegal or the partner's practice assistant what her preferences are. Some things you will learn by observing how the various people on the team interact with each other and work throughout the deal, so be sure to pay attention. By observing everyone's work style and adapting in little ways, you will make the lives of every single person on the deal easier, thus fulfilling the job of the junior associate: being of service.

If, for example, the partner you work with likes to review all of her materials on an iPad, don't bother printing anything out for her since she'll just throw it in the trash. Instead, make sure you send her one email, with all of the PDF files she needs clearly labeled so that she can access them and easily mark them up.

Maybe you hardly ever interact with the partner but report directly to a third-year associate. He might not seem that senior, but hierarchy means something in Biglaw, so you should figure out his work style, too. Ask him how he would like you to turn in your assignments. If you send him a 200-page document, should you also stop by with a hard copy? Little by little, you'll learn how everyone you work with likes to get things done and will be able to incorporate their preferences into your day.

2. Be Responsive and Communicative

We touched briefly on availability in the *Introduction* and a closely related topic, responsiveness, is just as important. Being responsive to senior attorney requests and client demands is essential for all Biglaw attorneys.

As a junior associate, you will be responsible for responding to your team members as close to immediately as possible (meaning, in the evenings and on weekends, too). This requirement never goes away in Biglaw, so be sure to learn its importance early on and accept that it is a part of Biglaw. It is not uncommon for a client to ask to speak to you out of the blue on a Saturday afternoon or request a call in the middle of the night because he is in another time zone . Biglaw is all about servicing the clients, so you better believe the partners are going to make those calls happen (however inconvenient they may be) when the client requests one.

Your primary role is to serve the senior lawyers on your team. Just as a partner would respond promptly to a client, respond to his questions and requests as soon as you can. Soon, you'll figure out when things are truly urgent and when they can wait a while, but when in doubt, respond and ask when the attorney is expecting your work product. It is always better to ask and receive a firm deadline than to assume something can wait. Be as communicative as possible, erring on the side of over-communication.

It should go without saying, but I'll note it quickly anyway just in case you skipped over the *Introduction*: in addition to responding to a task, you also need to be available to complete the task. The two go hand-in-hand. You must first respond, but the majority of what matters is your actual availability to do what is asked of you. Likewise, being available but not communicating that availability, or not responding that you are on top of a task, doesn't help anyone on the team. Senior associates and partners are juggling a lot more work than you are, so clearly communicating what you are doing is essential to keep things running smoothly.

3. Speak Up – At Appropriate Times

Lots of first-year associates feel intimidated, thinking about all of the things they don't know. If you start to feel like this, remember that you, too, are a lawyer. Even the most inexperienced lawyers have worked hard to get where they are and are super smart (that means you!), so they have something valuable to offer: their brains. Don't hesitate to share your opinion and question what is taking place; just do so at the appropriate time.

Speaking-up is a bit of a dance. While you shouldn't be a passive participant on your cases and deals, you also need to respect the Biglaw hierarchy. If you disagree with something a partner says, you absolutely should question it, but this calls for a lot of tact. Don't challenge a senior lawyer during a conference call or in front of a client, but do voice your opinion in private. Ask him why he said what he said. If you see an error in a document, point it out. Sometimes you won't be correct, but sometimes you will be. If you never voice your opinion, people may assume that you don't understand what is going on, don't care, or a combination of the two.

You usually can't go wrong if you speak up politely and professionally, and I'm sure you know how to do that, so there's not much point in telling you how. Instead, to make it abundantly clear, here's an example of what *not* to do. A first-year associate staffed on a Capital Markets deal was tasked with keeping track of the various documents and signature pages required for closing. It was a massive deal and the associate had taken it upon himself to learn more about the deal than just his minimal role required. So far, so good. Great, actually, because he was showing not only enthusiasm for his assignment but a genuine interest in the work.

Things started to go awry when the associate ran around frantically on the night before closing, first telling the mid-level associate and then the senior associate on the deal that the offered securities were not "fungible" (i.e., he had discovered a colossal tax issue that, if true, would have blown up the deal). Something got lost in translation and the senior associate thought that the tax partner, not the first-year associate, had raised the issue at the eleventh hour. It turned out, after the senior associate made a few frantic calls to the tax partner in the middle of the night, that the issue had been reviewed and analyzed by the tax experts ages ago, that the securities were, in fact, fungible, and the deal was clear to close.

This example illustrates a conundrum you might find yourself in. If you see an issue, perhaps even a deal-destroying one, you should raise it. Never stay silent and assume those more senior to you are correct just because they are senior to you or just because they are the experts. If something seems off, it's your duty to investigate why. Just don't emulate this associate in how you break the news. Make sure to be tactful and don't start a fire where the flame is of your own making. This associate was thereafter known among the lawyers of the group for this incident. While it was not career-destroying, it was certainly memorable, and not in a good way.

4. Be Prepared and Proactive

A junior associate might not always understand the nuances of a matter, but he can always be prepared for meetings and calls. Be the most prepared person on your team. Always have the relevant materials on-hand and ask ahead of time if you are unsure what to bring. You should never show up to a meeting, even if it's just a casual one with a mid-level associate, without the documents to be discussed and a notepad and pen. If you like to take notes on your iPad, you can use that, but never rely just on your phone. No matter how efficient you are with the notes app or whatever it is you use to take notes on your phone, scrolling through your phone, even if you are using it for work, looks totally unprofessional to those more senior to you.

Preparation also includes anticipation. Don't always wait for work to come to you. If you're staffed on an active matter and find yourself without work, go to all of the lawyers on your team and ask how you can help. Make it known that you have time and show that you are interested, available, and excited to work. Soon, being proactive might also mean taking it upon yourself to complete something even before it is assigned if you know it is something that will have to get done. Everyone appreciates a junior associate who is actively engaged and doesn't just sit around waiting for the work to come to her.

~ ~ ~

When you begin a Biglaw job, you are just one in the sea of many, but it doesn't take long to make yourself an integral and irreplaceable part of the team. To do so, you must provide value to the senior attorneys with whom you are working.

Working with senior attorneys, especially those who are set in their ways, can be intimidating at first. On top of your actual assignments, there is so much to learn when it comes to working with (and for) others. If you are adaptable, responsive and communicative, voice your opinion when and where appropriate, and are prepared and proactive, working with anyone at the firm, no matter who it is, won't seem so daunting anymore.

Chapter Two

Understanding Who Your Client Is

In the last chapter, we looked at what it means for junior associates to provide value to those they work for, namely the partners and any associate more senior to them. One crucial group of people was missing from most of that conversation. You're probably wondering, what about the clients?

In Biglaw, the client is king. They pay premium prices for Biglaw work and expect excellence and delivery of exactly what they've asked for. As a junior associate, especially during your first and second years, while you will work directly with clients, the majority of your deliverables will be filtered through one or more (and sometimes even many) levels of review before reaching the client.

That means that not only are the firm's clients your clients, but the internal lawyers (partners, counsel, and senior associates) who review your work are your clients, too. Let's take a look at the various clients a junior associate is likely to encounter, both internally and externally, as well as a third party who is not a client but who you should also keep in mind and cater to when drafting your work.

Senior Lawyers

In *Chapter One*, we talked about how to provide value to partners and other senior attorneys. Depending on the structure of your team, those lawyers, not the client, may be the only ones you work with directly. Because of this, they are, in essence, your first clients. Never provide sub-optimal work to someone internally because you know they will review it before it gets sent to a client. Treat whoever it is you turn your draft into as a paying client and produce the same quality work you would for that paying client.

At the same time, you shouldn't ignore who the ultimate client is (for more on how to cater your work to clients, see below) even when you don't have a direct line to them. If it is not apparent from the assignment, ask the senior lawyer who the assignment is for. Is the client a banker, a general counsel, or someone else? Knowing who the end client is will help you craft a better draft for review. For example, a partner's tone and style will be different if the work product is ultimately going to a CFO as opposed to a junior banker, so the draft you provide to the partner should reflect that. Tailoring your work to specific clients is a skill that takes time to develop, and you won't be great at changing tone and anticipating what the client wants right away, but you'll get the hang of it soon enough.

External Clients

Now we get to the good stuff: the external clients. They are the ones who pay the big bucks and expect excellent work product, which can create a lot of pressure. But, if you put the time into understanding who the client is, you can alleviate a lot of this pressure.

Of course, you will know who your client is, whether it is a bank, an investment manager, a pharmaceutical company, or any number of clients Biglaw firms routinely represent. However, understanding who the client is isn't enough; you must understand who the person (or people) is at the other end of your email, phone call, or document. Will a junior banker be receiving your spreadsheet? A general counsel who has to review documents you've asked him to sign? An assistant general counsel who needs to provide comments on a loan agreement? Those are very different people who should receive very different work product. Here's some more information on how you can provide that.

Level I: The Junior Banker (or any other junior-level person at a client)

As a junior associate, the most direct interaction you'll have with a client is most likely going to be with someone at a similarly junior level. This could be a junior banker, an assistant VP at a company, or any number of positions. The person will generally be your age or younger and not have much job experience. They will also probably work long hours since they, too, are new to the job and the field (this is especially true for young investment bankers). Understand what their job entails, how much they have on their plate, and tailor what you send to them accordingly. For example, most junior bankers don't like to receive or don't have time to read wordy emails or documents. In this case, send them your questions in a format they are used to, like a spreadsheet or a succinct, bullet-point list.

These are also great clients to develop a rapport with, and

even a true friendship in some cases, because they are probably your contemporaries and have a similar lifestyle, which can't be said for many other clients (e.g., a general counsel of a public company). Use this to your advantage and get to know them through your emails and late-night phone calls. As one partner I worked for used to say, one day those clients who are juniors when you are, too, will be managing directors and general counsels when you are a partner. Down the line, when you are looking for clients, the bonds and relationships you develop at the beginning of your career will carry through and bring you work when you need it later on.

Level II: The Associate General Counsel / Associate In-House Counsel (or any mid-level position at a client)

Mid-level in-house counsel and other mid-level corporate workers (such as finance officers or associates at a company) are the second-most typical client you'll interact with as a junior associate. Usually, these people have been at the job for a few years (some have been at their company for many, many years) and they report to the more senior people at their office.

What is the best way to approach a mid-level client? First, understand that you might be asking for a lot of their time and, second, make things as easy for them as possible. These can be tricky clients to work with because often you are asking them to do additional things on top of their day jobs. For example, if you are working on a loan agreement for the company, the assistant general counsel might be tasked with providing you all of the answers to your questions, gathering thousands of diligence documents you've asked to review, and reviewing all of the transaction documents.

All of this, on top of her day job.

How can you be the most helpful to an in-house counsel? Make her job easier. Instead of just giving in-house counsel a bulleted list of issues, provide her with the reasoning behind your list, along with a spreadsheet of the calculations backing up your analysis. This will help her both understand what you are asking of her so she can make a decision, and give her the back-up information she needs if her boss asks her about it. Her company will expect her to know the reasoning behind everything, so it is your task to educate her on this. Your ultimate job is to make her look good in front of her colleagues, so keep that in mind when working with these clients.

Level III: The General Counsel (or CFO, Board Member or any other high-up, decision maker at a client)

While you might have less direct contact with the general counsels, CFOs, presidents, and other senior management at a client, junior lawyers will still prepare draft work product which ultimately gets sent to the client by a more senior associate or partner. But don't think you won't have *any* contact with them, as it is often the most junior associate's job to chase these people down (either directly or with the assistance of their secretaries) to get their all-important signatures or sign off. So there will still be times where you will work directly with these higher-ups, even as a junior associate. Sometimes you will email or call them about substantive work, too; it all depends on the nature of the work and the team you are working with. It is best to be prepared to interact with these people, even if you don't end up doing so on day one, because as you rise up in the Biglaw ranks, you soon will.

What do these clients generally need from you? Simplicity and directness. They don't have time to review a 200-page document; they have time to review a list of ten bullet-points summarizing the document. They don't have time to sift through a long-winded email with twenty signature page attachments; they have time to read a one-sentence email explaining what you need from them with one attachment. You get the point. What they lack is time, so it is your job to provide them with all of the information they need, while taking up the least amount of their time.

These people are also the decision makers, so what you provide them will usually be issues they need to make a decision about. They are not paying you, though, just to list Option A and Option B: they want your advice, so you need to provide that advice (succinctly, of course). A good way to do this is to list out the pros and cons of every choice, as well as a recommended choice (if you have one). Remember, don't waste their time, and simplicity is key.

Lawyers on the Other Side

Lastly, there's a third type of "client" you should consider when preparing a draft, and that is the lawyer on the other side. On many matters, you will work far more often and more closely with lawyers from other Biglaw firms than you will with your own clients. These may be the lawyers representing the other side in a litigation or the company being acquired by your client in an M&A transaction.

While another law firm's lawyers are obviously not your client, they will be on the receiving end of your work product and you will be on the receiving end of theirs. What you give you will often get back, so make things easy for them to make things easy for yourself. How can you do this? Instead of sending out a document at 5:00 p.m. on a Friday, if you have it done earlier, send it out then. Nobody likes a Friday afternoon document dump, but you better believe that if you consistently do that to the other side, they will do it right back to you. You can also do little things like making sure documents you send out are clearly labeled and organized. Another courteous gesture is to give the other side a heads-up when you know something is coming down the pike. If you know lots of documents are about to come through in a few hours or their weekend will be consumed by what you are about to send, do the courteous thing and give them fair warning (so long as you aren't giving any strategy away). Chances are, they will do the same for you when the tables are turned.

Some associates at other law firms are total jerks and no matter how well you treat them or how respectful you are, they will treat you poorly whenever the opportunity arises. I found that most, however, were just like you and me: trying to get through the day and the Biglaw week without too much added stress while doing a great job for their clients. Especially with the type of work where you see the same firms and the same associates and partners deal after deal, having an ally on the other side pays off immensely. The bottom line is, do unto lawyers at other firms as you wish they would do unto you, and you will find yourself a much calmer and more respected lawyer.

~ ~ ~

Producing quality work product, tailored to the needs of your specific client, is how you gain the trust of your coworkers and your clients. As a lawyer, your ultimate goal, no matter what your actual Biglaw end goal is, is to become your client's "trusted advisor." A lot has been written about what it means to be a trusted advisor. For me, it boils down to (1) providing outstanding legal advice and (2) delivering that outstanding legal advice in a context that your client can digest and use in his business.

Learn early on in your career to always keep the client in mind: Who is he? What does he need? How much time does he have to review your work? How can you make him look good in front of his boss? The list goes on and on. If you do this, you will be well on your way to becoming a trusted advisor.

Chapter Three

Working With and Learning From People at All Levels

At every stage in your Biglaw career, you will gain valuable skills. Your first few years are a crash course. Junior associates in Biglaw are like sponges, absorbing this new world as best they can and gaining skills along the way. Over time, you will stop putting many of those skills to use because they will be applicable only to tasks done by those more junior to you. "Use it or lose it" is a very accurate phrase for much of what you learn in Biglaw. The Biglaw hierarchy is set up so that you can lose some of those skills as you replace them with new ones. The Biglaw machine will still run since new associates will be there to fill any and all gaps. Because of this, there is no one person, not even a partner, from whom you can learn all of the skills necessary to turn you into the very best attorney and successful Biglaw associate you can be.

To become a well-rounded associate, you must work directly with people at all levels across the firm so that you can learn from all types of people. Below are examples of the various groups of people all first-year associates will encounter and should make an effort to work with, and what skills you will likely learn from working with each one.

Paralegals

On your first day of Biglaw, paralegals will be your number one ally and number one resource. Paralegals in Biglaw know more than any junior associate possibly can about the inner workings of the firm. They fall into two camps: the career paralegals who are usually extremely knowledgeable in one specific area of the law (for example, they are the firm's expert at filing court documents in all jurisdictions) and the super-bright twenty-somethings, just out of college, who are working at the firm as their first-ever job. Both of these groups of paralegals can help you navigate the tricky issues you'll encounter as a junior associate. Let's start with the first group: the career paralegals.

Many career paralegals have been at their Biglaw firm for years. They work either for a specific group or for the entire firm, focusing on a niche area of the law. Don't be too afraid or too proud to ask them for help whenever you need it. They probably save junior associates from making colossal mistakes more than any other group of people at the firm. I know they sure saved me a couple of times.

When I was a junior associate, after a transaction had closed, it was my job to file a U.C.C. financing statement to secure the collateral for our client. I made the mistake of picking the wrong jurisdiction to file the collateral in, and when I sent the financing statement to the career paralegal to process and file, he asked me, "Are you *sure* you want to file in X jurisdiction and not Y jurisdiction?" It was his way of saying, "This is totally wrong; I'm not going to file it in X jurisdiction, but I'm going to teach you so that you learn from this and don't make the mistake again." I thanked him for pointing out my mistake before it was too late and you better believe I never made that mistake again. Thanks to him, the transaction was saved. Get to know these paralegals, the type of work they do, what support they can offer you, and what you can learn from them.

As for the more common, younger paralegal, they will be in the trenches with you at all hours and, in the beginning, will know more about the typical administrative tasks that junior associates are usually assigned than you will. Firms expect junior associates to know how to get certain things done without much guidance, so paralegals are often the ones you turn to in order to figure out how to get these things done. Here are some examples of things I would have had no idea how to get done without the help of the fantastic paralegals I worked with over the years:

- Putting together closing document sets in the exact way a client expects them to look.
- Knowing which grumpy employee at the courthouse will actually take your call and answer an urgent question on a Friday afternoon.
- Having a great relationship with the guys in the copy center so you can skip the line and pull off a giant printing job at the last minute, right before a huge client meeting.
- Knowing the home addresses of all the partners in your group and their preferred document delivery methods (sometimes partners like to have physical copies of things delivered to them at home, with precise instructions as to how they want those things delivered).

You might be wondering, what about the secretaries? Aren't

they often touted as the ones who know everything about the firm and don't you need one to have your back to succeed? I had heard this, too, but I don't think it's the case anymore. There was a time when secretaries (now usually called practice assistants) were essential administrative members of the team who could help you immensely and from whom you could learn a lot, too. However, that is mostly a relic of the past. While there are still some amazing practice assistants out there, they tend to do amazing work for the partners they have been working with for ten or twenty years, not for the junior associates.

While you will be assigned to work with a practice assistant when you begin work, in my experience, most practice assistants worked with multiple attorneys, and work for junior associates was definitely not their priority. Mostly, they will answer your phone during business hours and take your messages. For this reason, instead of assuming that your practice assistant will be the most valuable resource for all things related to the inner workings of the firm, know that it is much more likely that the paralegals will fill that role.

Second- and Third-Year Associates

If you are a first-year associate, summer associate, or haven't started your Biglaw career yet, the associates to seek out first for many of your questions will be the second- and third-year associates. They have recently been through what you are going through now and have come out on the other side. After years and years of working in Biglaw, a person becomes removed from the trials and tribulations of a lost and confused first-year associate. Seek out the advice and guidance of these associates whenever you can because they know what you're facing.

While you probably won't work directly with someone just one or two years your senior (in the sense that you will not turn your work into him for review), you will be working on teams with junior associates. These second- and third-year associates on your teams and with whom you share an office or a neighboring office can serve as your allies and confidants, and the ones to go to for advice on anything you are hesitant to ask someone more senior. They are your first line of questioning when you need to know things you don't want to ask a senior attorney, such as how to send a fax (surprisingly, this is sometimes still required) or how to document business trip-related expenses. If they don't know the answer to your question, at least you know it wasn't a dumb one and you can be more confident reaching out to someone more senior with the question.

I was staffed on a major M&A and bank regulatory transaction a month into my first year. It was an acquisition of a foreign bank by a U.S. bank, so it involved both complex M&A and bank regulatory aspects. It was high-paced, demanding, and intense. The most valuable lessons I learned on that deal came from the second-year associate I worked closely with, not from the partners on the deal who were (and are) some of the most powerful partners at the firm. I learned how to book a town car to take me home late at night (this was pre-Uber), how to order dinner at my desk, what kind of supplies I should keep at the office for those super late nights (extra sweatpants because it turns out it *is* appropriate to change out of your business casual attire past a certain time at night), and how to "print" a document to PDF so it could be electronically signed.

Mid-Level Associates

The definition is not set in stone, but an associate generally transitions from junior associate to mid-level associate when she reaches her fourth year or so at the firm, and she will stay at this level for about three years (her fourth, fifth, and sixth years at the firm). By this time, she will have spent enough time at the firm and as a practicing attorney to understand the substantive aspects of the work.

Mid-level associates can serve as great teachers and mentors to those starting out. They have new-found knowledge and confidence and will be eager to share that knowledge with anyone who wants to learn it. Aside from teaching you something like the process of filing a document in a litigation or the mechanics of a closing, they can explain *why* you are doing what you are doing, what the purpose of your task is, and how it fits into the larger picture of the matter. While these associates may not yet grasp the nuances of every filing or transaction document, they will still be able to provide you with an excellent overview.

How should you take advantage of working with a mid-level associate and what can you learn from her? You should be able to ask a mid-level associate as many questions as you want, without feeling stupid or like you are wasting her time. A good mid-level associate will be able to give you answers to most of your questions and, if she does not know the answer, will be comfortable saying something like: "I'm not sure, let's ask a partner" or "We have to table that question for now because we have to turn to something more urgent." The best mid-level associate to work with is one who is both confident in her work and confident enough to know what she does *not* know.

Senior Associates

Similar to the definition of a mid-level associate, the definition of a senior associate is somewhat ambiguous, but it is generally defined as an associate who is a seventh-year associate and up. These associates are senior enough to competently answer almost all of your questions and explain the reasoning behind all of your assignments. At the same time, they are not *so* many years removed from being a first-year associate that they still have some understanding of what it was like to be a junior associate and what a junior associate should be expected to know and understand. A good senior associate will be able to answer almost all of your substantive legal questions as well as a partner could. A great one will sit down with you and explain your assignments to you and make you feel welcome enough to continue to ask him questions throughout your time working together.

If you are genuinely interested in learning about the law, I found senior associates to be some of the most valuable people at the firm to learn from. While partners have more experience and more legal knowledge than senior associates, even the most engaged partners who truly want associates to succeed have trouble remembering what exactly a first-year or a second-year associate understands. They've just been out of the trenches for way too long to be able to remember what it was like to be a junior associate, so they forget what your abilities are. Senior associates were in your shoes not that long ago, so they can better tailor their explanations and assignments to what you can understand and to your abilities.

Senior associates also have a lot of control over who gets

staffed on what, and what specific assignments everyone on a team gets. By growing close to and doing great work for a senior associate, you'll also give yourself access to better assignments, which allows you to keep on learning from these valuable teachers.

Partners

A partner needs little to no introduction. He's been at the firm for many years, and between client work and firm responsibilities, he has a lot on his plate. For this reason, a partner who is willing to work directly with a first- or second-year associate can be hard to find. Mostly, this is not because partners don't want to work with junior lawyers but rather because they simply don't have the time to devote to all of the teaching that needs to be done when working with junior associates. If you do get the chance to work directly with a partner, seize that opportunity. You might feel like a chicken with your head cut off when he talks to you, but the opportunity to learn case strategy and deal structure directly from a partner is invaluable.

When I was a second-year associate, I was the most senior associate staffed on a deal. It began as something relatively small and morphed into an absolutely massive deal. The partner and I worked together for hours on end, every day, for months. There were so many things on this transaction that I, as an inexperienced second-year associate, could not have anticipated and that the partner had long forgotten how to solve, since these were usually taken care of by the mid-level or senior associates.

While we probably could have avoided many of the issues that popped up if there had been a mid-level or senior associate on the deal, the knowledge I gained on that deal was invaluable. I got to do work that was way above my head and that I would never have had the chance to do had I not been working directly with the partner. The partner later told me that throwing me into this transaction felt somewhat like taking his ten-year-old kid to an R-rated movie too soon! But we (both) survived and formed a bond that would last throughout my career at the firm and beyond. Not only that, but the client we represented remained with me for my entire time at the firm and eventually even became my favorite client to work for.

You might not have as big an assignment with a partner as I just described or develop as close a working relationship with one so early in your career, but you will inevitably get the opportunity to work one-on-one with a partner at some point. Even if you just get to sit in on conference calls with a partner, you can learn so much from him. And don't forget that he can learn from you, too. As I noted in *Chapter One*, part of adding value as a junior associate is sharing your opinion. If you are the only one in the room during a call with a partner, take advantage of the fact that you are the only other opinion he has. If you have a different interpretation of something mentioned on the call, you should share it. Even partners don't know everything and make mistakes (which we'll talk more about in *Chapter Eight*). You'll learn from them and the good ones will learn from you, too.

~ ~ ~

Working with a mix of people in Biglaw will fast-track your learning and ultimately benefit your career. Be strategic about who you work with to make sure you expose yourself to a diverse group of people and knowledge. Seek to expand who you work with and learn from because working with different people brings you different perspectives, shows you different working styles, and, most importantly, gives you the required skills you need to succeed in Biglaw.

Chapter Four

The Importance of Finding Both Mentors and Sponsors

Surrounding yourself with people to guide you, listen to you, offer advice, and advocate for you, is essential if you want to succeed in Biglaw. You've hopefully had people like this throughout your life, and you'll need them throughout your Biglaw life, too. You probably think I'm talking about finding a mentor, which I am, but I'm also talking about finding a sponsor, which you'll also need if you want to go far in Biglaw.

What exactly are mentors and sponsors, and what's the difference? In a nutshell, a mentor offers you guidance, advice, and support, while a sponsor advocates for you, champions you, and helps you advance in your career. Mentors and sponsors can be the same person, but aren't always. Some sponsors start out as mentors only and evolve into sponsors as your working relationship grows.

Mentors offer advice from the perspective of someone who has been there before. They might be other lawyers at your firm or someone outside of your Biglaw world, such as a favorite college professor or a former law school classmate. Sponsors, on the other hand, have a seat at the table: they are the decision makers. In short, in Biglaw, they are the partners.

Let's dive into the details of and the differences between the two, and then we'll discuss why it's so vital to cultivate each type of relationship during your Biglaw career. In Biglaw, these are the key qualities that you will find in a mentor and a sponsor:

MENTORS	SPONSORS
Mentors have mentees.	Sponsors have proteges.
Mentors have experience in a specific area that you need advice about. They are people within your organization, such as other associates or partners, or outside of it, such as alumni from your law school or lawyers at local bar associations.	Sponsors hold senior positions in your *own* organization. In Biglaw, an associate's sponsor will likely be the partner you work closest with throughout your career and who champions you when you are up for partnership.
Mentors are not necessarily personally invested in a mentee's career success. Think of them as friendly big brothers or big sisters who take you under their wing and show you the ropes.	Sponsors *are* professionally invested in their protege's career success. A protege's success will benefit the sponsor. In Biglaw, a partner will sponsor an associate who has the potential to bring in business down the line and who will be a successful partner.

Mentors	Sponsors
Mentors offer informal support on topics such as navigating assignments, workplace politics, and personal issues.	Sponsors actively promote their proteges and build up their reputations among other partners and firm stakeholders.
Mentors advise mentees about expanding their networks and learning of new opportunities within the firm or in the outside legal world.	Sponsors connect proteges with influential people within the firm and among the firm's clients. They take proteges to client meetings and help them develop their networks and books of business early on.
Mentors offer advice on what assignments to take, which lawyers to work with, and how to get the work that you want.	Sponsors usually work directly with proteges, giving them assignments with prime clients and letting them take the lead on client work to gain visibility within the firm and among clients.
Mentors share firm "secrets" and unwritten rules, like which partner is respectful and who is a nightmare to work for.	Sponsors share the inner workings of the firm with their proteges, revealing the business side of Biglaw, such as client billing practices and partner compensation.
Mentors prepare mentees for survival in Biglaw or wherever they choose to take their legal careers.	Sponsors prepare proteges for the ultimate goal: partnership.

For junior Biglaw attorneys, mentors are both easier to come by and more necessary at this point in your career. Mentors will make you better at your job and will help you figure out what job is right for you. Because sponsors are directly invested in their proteges' advancement and put their own necks on the line by providing them with connections and prime work, a sponsor-protege relationship does not usually solidify until an associate reaches his fifth year or so at the firm (at the earliest). However, it is important to keep the concept of sponsors in the back of your mind from day one. By the time you become a senior associate and are considering trying to make partner, you need to have someone backing you and championing you among the partnership. Having both mentors and sponsors throughout your Biglaw career can mean the difference between fizzling out after a few years and making partner.

Not only can you have more than one mentor, but I would also encourage that. I had many mentors over the course of my Biglaw career (but only one sponsor). Some of these mentors I got to know in passing and some stuck around the whole time; some I worked with directly and others I did not. Here's how to find both a mentor and a sponsor, and how you can best take advantage of both types of relationships.

How to Find a Mentor (Or Many)

Almost anyone can be a mentor. You can have one mentor for one aspect of your career and another for something else. You can have one mentor you actively seek out, one that becomes one because you work together so frequently, or one that was assigned to you through some sort of firm program. Here are common ways for

Biglaw junior associates to find helpful mentors.

1. Work With Someone Who Naturally Becomes Your Mentor

A great way to find a mentor is to let the relationship develop between you and someone you work with naturally. This mentor is usually a mid-level or senior associate with whom you work well and on a consistent basis. This is how most of my mentorship relationships at the firm began. This is not the most proactive way to find a mentor and it only works if you consistently work for associates with whom you get along (if you can't find consistent work from someone you enjoy working with, you probably have bigger issues and questions to ask yourself about your time at that firm or in Biglaw).

It also takes time to develop this kind of mentorship relationship. You cannot work with someone for one week and magically become her mentee. It takes time but it's worth it and some of the best mentorship relationships develop this way.

2. Seek One Out

If you want to be more proactive in finding a mentor, strategically seek one out. Look for someone you would like to emulate, who seems like she has it all together, who has been in your shoes before, who is in a career path you would like to pursue in the future, or who seems interested in sharing her knowledge with others. These are just a few examples of people you can seek out as mentors. If you feel comfortable doing so, you can ask someone straight-up if they'd be willing to be your mentor. If not, you can start the relationship by asking them to coffee, lunch, or a meet-up to chat and get to know each other. It does not have to be called a mentorship relationship to be one.

Anyone can serve as a mentor. Here are a few of the places you can look to as a junior associate to find a mentor:

- Associates at your firm: whether they are in your practice group, a practice group you are interested in, or not, other associates should be your first stop when searching for a mentor. Associates can offer advice on firm-specific things like how to navigate too much work or how to work with a notoriously demanding partner.
- Your law school alumni network: alumni can offer advice on things like how to get a job in another city, they can review your resumé, they can give you tips on interviewing for in-house roles, and more.
- Legal organizations and bar associations in your city: members can offer advice on doing pro bono work, introduce you to practitioners who work in-house, and connect you with those working in your field.
- Your law school classmates: your classmates who were 2Ls or 3Ls when you were a 1L are great resources, offering similar advice to associates at your firm, but with an outside perspective.

3. Let the Firm Find One for You

My least favorite, but the most common, form of mentorship is the firm's formal mentorship program. I can't tell you how many mentors and, later on, mentees, I was assigned throughout my Biglaw career. From the partner mentor I had as a summer associate who I never met because he was so busy traveling for work to the summer associate mentees I "mentored" (which involved taking them out to drinks one time over the summer), I was in a countless number of these mentorship programs. Especially as a junior associate, I'm pretty sure I was never *not* in some sort of mentorship group, circle, pairing, or whatever it was called at the moment.

I don't want to deter you from participating in these programs, as I found them to be fun and a great way to meet other lawyers at the firm who I normally never would have interacted with. Just don't get your hopes up that you will be assigned a mentor who will guide you throughout your career. More likely, you will be assigned someone in a practice group you are not interested in just because you happened to go to the same law school fifteen years apart. Other than bonding over the school's football team, you might not have much in common in terms of where you are in your career or your life.

While firms are getting better at creating more effective mentoring programs, they can still feel very forced and are not the best way to find an actual mentor. That being said, you might get lucky and get assigned a mentor who is a match and a great resource. If nothing else, you'll meet some new people and hopefully make some friends. Participate in these programs; just keep your expectations low.

How to Successfully Use the Mentorship Relationship to Benefit Both Parties

Traditionally, a mentorship relationship benefits the mentee. However, it is not just a one-way street. In a good mentorship relationship, a mentor learns and receives a benefit, too. Here's how you can make sure your mentorship relationship thrives and benefits both the mentee and the mentor.

1. Take Charge and Organize Your Meet-Ups

Mentors are often busier than mentees. They might mentor more than one person on top of an already hectic work schedule. Do everything you can to make it easy for them to mentor you. Be the one who sets the meetings, who follows up when they forget about a call, and who is accommodating to their schedule, not the other way around. Even well-intentioned mentors sometimes need a little prodding, so take charge.

2. Come Prepared With Questions

Don't just show up at your mentor's doorstep and expect to be guided. You have to ask for what you want; otherwise, you won't get the advice you need or, even worse, you won't get any advice at all. If you don't come prepared, your mentor may assume you don't want to be there and the relationship may peter out before it even gets going. Ask the right questions to the right mentors. It's worthwhile to have more than one mentor, as it is unlikely that one person can serve as your guide throughout your whole Biglaw career or across every aspect of it.

3. Put Their Feedback to Use

Mentors want to know that you are not wasting their time. Of course, you don't have to take all of their advice and nobody expects you to, but you should take their feedback and let them know what you did with it. Did you follow their advice? If so, how did things turn out? Did you decide to take a different approach?

They want to know this, too, as it will help them guide you later on.

Most importantly, show them that you take the relationship and their time seriously by actively making moves instead of passively waiting for things to happen to you. Don't go to them with the same problem over and over again, without doing anything about it to make a change. Show your mentor that you are someone worth investing in.

4. Do Great Work for Them

If your mentor is someone you work with, whether he's an associate or partner, the best way you can repay the favor of his mentorship and guidance is simply by doing great work. By guiding you and helping you become the best at your job as you possibly can, they will reap the benefits, too. Show them that you are worth their time by making their lives easier and becoming the best Biglaw associate you can be (for tips on how to do just that, see *Chapters One* through *Three* and *Five* through *Twenty-Five*!).

5. Don't Be Afraid to Offer Advice

Just because you are a junior lawyer does not in any way mean that you don't have advice to offer, too. A mentorship relationship might begin as mentor to mentee, but sometimes the mentee can become the mentor, too. If the relationship becomes more of a mutual one, with both parties sharing information and advice, it can benefit everyone. It is also more likely to last and you'll develop a stronger bond, which benefits both the mentor and the mentee.

How to Find a Sponsor

A sponsor is your advocate on the inside. He shows you the steps needed to take your career to the next level – to partnership – and helps you get there. A partner-sponsor raises your visibility within the firm among partners who otherwise would never know your name, but whose votes you need to become one of them.

Even though I did not stick it out in Biglaw long enough to try for partnership, I was fortunate enough to have had a sponsor, even though, for most of my career, I didn't know what a sponsor was. By the time I was a sixth-year associate or so, I knew that I had someone in my corner who would advocate on my behalf for partnership if the time came. While partnership wasn't guaranteed, I had access to the best deals, prime clients, and my name was floated around the firm as someone with potential.

Mentors can show you the ropes as a junior associate, but no mentorship relationship can get you to partnership. Only a sponsor can do that. Unfortunately, it is often noted that women and minorities are likely to have just as many mentors as white men but not as many sponsors. To advance to partnership, a sponsor is what you need, so this gap needs to be bridged. That's a topic for another time, but be aware of the statistic so you can put in extra effort if you need to in order to find a sponsor who will be your advocate. One probably won't fall into your lap (no matter who you are).

Your firm will undoubtedly have a mentorship program. It is less likely that your firm will have a formal sponsorship program, but check with HR to see if there is something. If there is one, it is probably for more senior associates who have already proven their worth, but keep it in mind for the future. Finding a sponsor is not as simple as finding a mentor, but you can start to cultivate a sponsorship relationship long before you reach the ranks of senior associate. Here's how.

1. Identify Potential Sponsors

Just as not every associate is cut out for partnership, not every partner has what it takes to be a sponsor or is even interested in being one. That's why it's crucial to identify potential sponsors early on in your career so you know which partners could potentially play that part for you. Key questions to ask yourself when evaluating whether a partner has the potential to be your sponsor include:

- Does he have a leadership role within the firm or your practice group?
- Does he seem well-regarded by other partners in the firm and your practice group?
- Does he have a history of promoting associates within the firm to partner?
- Does he seem devoted to the firm (i.e., he is unlikely to leave the firm for another one)?
- Does he have a large book of business, and he needs or will need junior partners to share that business with soon?
- Does he take an interest in working with associates or does he only speak with clients and other partners?
- Does he seem to participate in firm events and committees, such as the firm's summer associate committee or mentorship programs (a partner who shows interest in associate

development is more likely to show interest in sponsorship, too)?

- Does he work with both male and female associates, equally, as well as with those from diverse backgrounds? If not, unless you happen to look just like him, he might not be open to sponsoring you (as hard of a pill to swallow as that might be).

None of these factors, on its own, guarantees a certain partner would be willing to serve as a sponsor, just as a lack of any or all of these is not dispositive of someone's willingness or ability to serve in that role. Remember, sponsorship is mutual – it benefits the partners, too – so it is in their best interest to sponsor promising junior associates. Not all partners have gotten that memo yet, but most of the good ones have.

Also look for someone in your own niche. He doesn't necessarily have to be in your office (especially if your office is not the hub for that specific practice area). If there is someone who you think would sponsor you in the future, begin to cultivate that relationship now. Do great work for them. Join their pro bono projects and their firm committees. Tell them about your career ambitions. Let them know that you are in this for the long haul (if you are) and don't be shy about your goal of partnership. Partners love associates who want to be partners, so tell them if that's something you want. If you know a long-term Biglaw career is something you want, identify potential sponsors, and reach out to them early on.

2. Ask About Your Firm's Sponsorship Programs

Does your firm have some sort of sponsorship program that you could participate in? As a junior associate, you probably won't be eligible to participate in it yet, but know what type of formal programs are in place for the future. If nothing exists, talk to HR about it. By the time you are a senior associate, the firm might have put one in place, but is unlikely to do so unless people ask for it.

Formal sponsorship programs can be worthwhile. Be aware that some of the sponsorship programs in Biglaw might be called mentorship programs, but you will be able to tell the difference. If they are aimed at high-achieving, senior-level associates, and are one-on-one pairings (as opposed to a mentorship circle or group) with partners in your own practice group, they are more likely to be sponsorship programs than not.

3. Develop a Quality Relationship With a Partner That Goes Beyond Doing Great Work

Like mentorship relationships, sponsorships that happen organically between a partner and associate who work together repeatedly and for many years are the most valuable and strongest ones. Once you've identified a potential partner-sponsor or you find one through luck, continue to develop your bond with that partner.

Sponsors are advocates who put their own reputations on the line for their proteges, which means you have to build up a lot of trust. The best way to do that is to do great work and to be exceptionally reliable, mature, and diligent. You should also get to know your sponsor on a more personal level, as that's how the trust really develops. Take the time to learn about their interests, their families, and what makes them tick, and they should do the same for you. After all, they are hopefully sponsoring you and inviting you into the partnership, so trust will make them feel comfortable doing that.

How to Successfully Use the Sponsorship Relationship to Benefit Both Parties

By definition, a sponsorship relationship is symbiotic. An associate receives insight and access into the partnership, while the partner gets the support and hard work of a devoted associate (and potential partner).

You do not owe your sponsor anything if you decide you do not want to stay at the firm. That's the risk they take in sponsoring you. But you do owe them your 100% devotion to the firm while you are there. If you are granted access and privileges other associates are not, it is your job to step up and show that you deserve this special treatment. Prove that you've earned it by working harder than you've ever worked before and showing that you are a leader. No longer is it enough to show that you are a good associate and team player, you must also show that you can lead. This might mean stepping up and juggling more than you think you can, managing more associates, or dealing with demanding clients. In return, you will, hopefully, become a partner, so act like one before you become one.

~ ~ ~

Mentorship and sponsorship relationships are essential to your success as a junior associate. While some of these relationships will develop naturally and over time, and those are usually the strongest and most worthwhile ones, sometimes you need to take action to make them happen. Seek out those people with more experience and more influence so you can make your Biglaw career what you want it to be. And don't forget to repay the gesture when you can. Even as a junior associate, there are opportunities for you to mentor others everywhere you look, from paralegals seeking advice about law school, to summer associates, to your college roommate changing careers, so step up and share your knowledge and experience with them.

Chapter Five

Don't "Delegate Up" or Take Advantage of Someone's Kindness

For many first-year associates (myself included), your Biglaw job is your first "real" job ever. With this job comes a lot of responsibility, which you might not be used to having. Inexperience, combined with a lack of substantive legal knowledge, might lead you to shirk your responsibilities or place the responsibility for your work on someone else. Don't succumb to either of these crutches.

You must act like a lawyer, no matter how little you might feel like one at times, and part of acting the part involves being responsible. There are two key ways this comes up during your junior associate years: (1) keeping your team in the loop while remaining responsible for your work (i.e., never "delegating up") and (2) not taking advantage of a nice senior associate or partner. Let's dive into both of these and explain how being responsible and taking ownership (there's that all-important Biglaw word again!) will help you succeed as a junior associate.

Keep Your Team in the Loop Without "Delegating Up"

You might not always feel competent, but your clients and lawyers on the other side of a transaction or litigation will expect you to know things. Legal things. As a junior associate, you won't always have all of the answers, and there's nothing wrong with that. In fact, it's expected! What is important is that you make sure you keep others on your team in the loop about what is going on so they can lend a hand when needed. If you are the only person on your team with a piece of information, make sure to share it with the appropriate members of your team. You never want to be the only person with knowledge of something.

For example, as the most junior associate on a project, one of your main tasks will probably be to send out mass emails. These may go out to your client, the other side, their attorneys, and third parties such as accountants and consultants, and they usually require responses or action from those various parties. Even if you have no idea what the documents you are sending out contain, or you didn't understand the email you yourself sent (sometimes a senior person will draft an email for you and ask you to send it), your recipients will not know this. If they have a comment or question about the email or the documents you just distributed, they will assume you, as the sender, are the proper person to ask.

Here's what works well when you find yourself on the receiving end of something you don't know how to handle.

1. Pass on Information to Your Team – Without Delegating Up

At the most basic level, it is your job as the junior associate to keep track of emails, questions, and responses that come in and to pass this information along to others on your team. This does not, however, mean that your job is simply to funnel the information or questions up to the senior members of your team and leave it at that.

Forwarding emails, issues, and problems to others on your team, without offering any support or solutions, is one of the most annoying things a junior associate can do. It is what was known (not affectionally) by a partner I worked for as "delegating up." While delegating up is better than ignoring something altogether, simply forwarding questions up the chain without thinking through the issue yourself comes in a close second.

What should you do if a question comes in that is above your head? Forwarding an issue to someone your senior and writing "see below" is not what firms pay you six figures to do. Instead, spend some time thinking about it, come up with your own ideas or answers, and be prepared to discuss the question with the senior associate or partner. Then, pass along the information.

If an email is addressed to you, it is your responsibility to answer it, or make sure somebody answers it, no matter how complex the question or the request. Even if there is a fourth-year associate or partner copied on an email addressed to you, *you* still need to be the one to respond. If you need to, you can reach out to the senior attorney to ask her to explain the answer to you. She might chime in and respond herself, but at the very least, you are in charge of keeping track of what needs to get done and ensuring that those who can answer the request are aware of it, are acting on it, or are directing you to act. There is nothing wrong with asking for help so long as you understand that the ultimate responsibility for solving the issue rests on your shoulders.

2. Loop Your Team in on Your Emails

Another way to provide value is by keeping your team in the loop on any correspondence you have. A good rule of thumb is to keep at least one person who is senior to you copied on basically all correspondence you are a part of (it is not necessary to do this for minor things, but as a junior associate it is hard to know what is minor, so err on the side of over-inclusion).

If someone emails only you with a question about something you do know the answer to, after you have discussed the issue internally and have figured out a proper response, respond and copy in your senior team member on that response. It is better to copy someone in from the beginning of the chain so that if an issue arises a few emails down the line, she has been a part of the chain and has access to it. This way, you won't have to fill her in on a few days' worth of correspondence at the last minute.

You also never know when someone more senior might spot an issue way before you would have spotted it, so it's good practice to give her the opportunity to do so by including her on all of your correspondence. As a senior associate, I liked to see how the deal was flowing and how all the moving pieces were fitting together and getting done. Being copied even on small matters gave me comfort that we were all on the same page and were on track.

3. Check in With Your Team in Person, Too

Not everything you do at work will be done via email (although sometimes it feels like that). You may talk to your clients on the phone or meet with a partner in person without other members of your team. A good practice is to make sure you share all of the information you take in with all of the parties on your team. This might mean summarizing your conversations in one email to send to the rest of the team at the end of the day or stopping by the senior associate's office every morning for a check-in meeting. You'll figure out a flow to this and what works for you, but the goal is never to be the only person with a piece of valuable information.

Keeping in constant communication with your coworkers will also come in handy when you want to take a vacation (see *Chapter Sixteen* on the art of taking vacation in Biglaw). The more team members in the loop and aware of what you are doing, the better someone will be able to cover for you when you are out of the office.

Don't Take Advantage of the Nice Seniors

Another way to be responsible for yourself and your work is by never taking advantage of nice, kind, or compassionate senior associates or partners. By the time I became a senior associate, I knew I was not perfect, but I also knew I was one of the good ones. The deals my group worked on were demanding, but I made a special effort to stay kind and empathetic no matter what. Not once in my career did I ever yell at someone, blame a mistake on a junior associate, or set unreasonable, arbitrary deadlines, and for this I am very proud. Did I know the most of any associate? No way. Did I work on the firm's sexiest deals? Definitely not. Did I bill the most hours? Nope. But if you were a junior associate who worked with me, you knew that you would also be treated with respect. This is why respect was basically all I asked for in return, and when I did not get it, I felt extremely let down.

The most common way a junior associate disrespects a senior associate is by treating her work as "less than." Resist the temptation to put the work of genuinely nice and respectful associates on the backburner in favor of someone else, be it an associate or a partner, who happens to be demanding, scary, mean, aggressive, or any combination of those things.

I cannot tell you the number of times a junior associate sat in my office and said, "I have to do X task for Rob," waiting for me to jump in and excuse her from the assignment I was about to give her. She expected me to know that because Rob was mean, she obviously had to complete his work first. Sometimes a junior associate would just say, "I have to do this for Rob," and no matter how urgent my assignment was, it was assumed that his work was more urgent than mine.

If the associate had allowed me to have a conversation about what she had on her plate, I am sure some of the times Rob's work should have taken priority, but I can guarantee it would not have been 100% of the time. Never giving me the opportunity to be the first choice was not the right thing to do. I could have handled it differently and told the junior associate "no" or pushed back, but I viewed her response as an example of how she would act going forward, so I simply wouldn't staff her again. I didn't have the time or the desire to work with someone who I had to teach how to respect others. There are plenty of junior associates to go around and every mid-level, senior, and partner will choose the one who puts his or her work first, hands down.

~ ~ ~

Being a responsible and respectful junior associate means you make your team aware of the work you are doing. It means staying on top of your work, thinking through issues before asking for help, and never just funneling information to others and "delegating up." You should strive to be an issue solver, not just an issue spotter. Always keep your team in the loop by copying them on emails and having regular check-ins. Remember also to respect the nice seniors just as much as you fear the mean ones. Never prioritize an assignment out of fear – prioritize your work based on the actual urgency of the tasks.

Chapter Six

Deciphering the Meaning of "My Door Is Always Open"

If you are a law student participating in OCI or an associate who has already gone through that process, you will inevitably have heard every single interviewer proudly state that his firm has an "open door policy." If you were anything like I was as a law student, you probably smiled, nodded, and wondered to yourself what he meant. You could tell by the tone of his voice that it was a good thing, but what did it really mean? The interviewer would go on to explain that even the busiest and most high-ranking partners at the firm leave their doors open, indicating that they are welcoming and available for drop-in visits at all times.

Most interviewers make Biglaw sound like a place where people are always flowing in and out of offices, discussing ideas, and asking questions. A place where an interruption for a quick chat or a lengthy legal debate is always welcome. That, however, is not what an open door policy means in Biglaw. *This* is what it means.

What Is an "Open Door" Policy?

The truth behind Biglaw's seemingly universal open door policy is that while, yes, many people do leave their office doors open, the phrase is more of a marketing tool that every interviewer (myself included when I used to interview potential associates) uses to paint her firm in the best light. Doors may be open, but everyone at a law firm is extremely busy. Senior attorneys may *want* to discuss issues and questions with you, but there is often not enough time. Even the senior attorneys who are the most generous with their time do not follow a true open door policy because, if they did, they would never be able to get anything done!

Knowing this, how can you get your questions answered while remaining a respectful junior associate? It is all about timing, preparation, and being strategic with your questions.

The Art of Asking a Question

Here are a few tips on how to get your questions answered without interrupting your colleagues, being seen as lazy, or asking the wrong person the wrong question.

1. Ask Urgent Questions in Person

There will be times, probably every day, where you will need an answer to a question ASAP. Whether a client has called with an urgent request that you need to track the partner down to fulfill or a filing deadline is fast approaching and you haven't received the partner's feedback yet, there will come a time where you need to go to a senior attorney's office and ask for a few minutes of her time.

Try to save these interruptions for when you truly need feedback urgently. This is also a good time to point out that if a question is urgent, don't send an email. If the person you need to contact is in her office, go to her office in person to discuss. If she isn't around or isn't available when you stop by her office, give her a call. This is *not* the time to send an email. Emails get lost in the shuffle or left for the end of the day, and if you need an answer now, sending an email is not the way to get that answer. This is the time to ask your question in person and keep on trying until you get the person's attention and answer.

2. Schedule Time to Ask More In-Depth Questions

While there will be plenty of opportunities to drop by someone's office to chat, especially once you've developed a good working relationship, you will not get as much value out of the interaction if you ambush someone with a question than if you were to schedule a time where he can devote his full attention to your questions.

One way to respect everyone's time is to schedule a brief check-in meeting first thing in the morning with an associate or partner you're working with (when possible, it's usually best to catch someone early in the day before they launch into endless calls and meetings and no longer have time for you). Gather together your questions, think through the issues, and then go to the senior associate or partner and sit down with him when he has time to discuss them with you. Not only will the senior attorney appreciate your preparedness and respect for his time, but you will get more out of the interaction, too.

3. Don't Be So Intimidated That You Never Ask Questions

On the other end of the spectrum, please don't be too scared or intimidated to approach a senior lawyer and don't take my previous advice to the extreme and *never* ask questions. An open door policy is all about finding the balance between stopping by unannounced and planning meetings ahead of time. If you choose to do neither and ask too few questions, it never ends well. Not asking any questions is way worse than asking too many. If you are too afraid or proud to ask someone a question, or you struggle through an assignment alone, get the assignment totally wrong, and bring a terrible work product to a senior associate, you are not doing anyone any favors.

If you don't understand something or need more clarification, don't leave someone's office until you 100% understand the assignment. Taking up more time on the front-end is preferable to screwing something up because you didn't understand your assignment and didn't ask enough questions to clarify it, so it has to be redone anyway.

4. There Is Such a Thing as a Dumb Question

There is absolutely such a thing as a dumb question. And you know what? You will have plenty of them. So what are you supposed to do? Well, there are two types of dumb questions in Biglaw: ones that you can't ask anyone, and ones that you can.

The first type of dumb questions are those that you want to ask because you are too lazy or tired to figure out the answer on your own, even though you are capable of doing so. Unless you are in an absolute time-crunch and have no time to figure it out yourself, don't ask anyone these questions. Part of your job as a junior associate is to work your way through issues and figure things out as you go. If you constantly bypass this step, you won't build the foundation you need to succeed, and you'll tick off your bosses along the way.

The second type of dumb questions are the ones that make you *feel* dumb, but aren't really. These are the ones mentioned in *Chapter Three* in the section about learning from second- and third-year associates. These questions are only dumb if you direct them to the wrong person. For example, there's no way a brand-new associate would know, without being told, how to do certain things like printing out a document in a specific format that the partner requires. How to get that done correctly is a valid question, but make sure you ask the right person (the copy center workers, the paralegal in your group, etc.) and not the wrong one (the partner). Use your common sense here and, when in doubt, lean on your fellow junior associates for guidance.

Asking Too Many Questions Isn't Good for Anyone

We talked about how to ask questions, but there's something else we have to address. There is such a thing as asking *too* many questions, even valid ones. Some lawyers, partners included, will really have open doors. Unless they are on the phone or in a meeting, they will be available to spend time with you, teach you, answer your questions, and work alongside you. If you find one of these lawyers, especially a partner, and enjoy their work and working with them, they are wonderful people to learn from.

This type of working relationship, however, can be detrimental to both your growth and the partner's. On your part, if you lean too heavily on the support of a partner and her willingness (although very much appreciated) to always be available to answer your questions and save you from struggling, you won't grow as much as you should. It is nice to have access to senior attorneys when you need it, but you also need time and space to learn and grow on your own, so be wary of senior attorneys who give too much of their time and too much support, as it might stifle your development.

Devoting so much time to working with you and being there to answer your questions can hinder a partner's work and growth, too. For example, one partner I knew would sit in her office with an associate, going over documents, comments, and questions, for hours on end. While this was helpful to the associates she worked with, it was ultimately detrimental to getting the work done efficiently because she never had enough time to complete her own work within a reasonable amount of time. It is one thing to teach and to be available, but it is another thing to do this at the expense of getting your work done. I mention this anecdote more for you to tuck away and remember as you advance in your career so that when you become a senior associate, you won't repeat this practice. As with many things in Biglaw, you must try to strike a balance, for everyone's sake.

~ ~ ~

What does Biglaw's open door policy mean? It means that there are times when associates are free to ask questions of even the most senior partners at the firm, but it doesn't mean that you have free rein to ask questions whenever it suits you. Respect the senior attorneys' time by asking urgent questions when necessary, scheduling time for more in-depth questions, and asking the right people the right questions. Don't be too scared or intimidated to ask a question or ask for clarification because asking is always better than doing something wrong. If a senior attorney is giving you a lot of her time, take it, but don't take advantage of it: it will only hurt your development. Asking questions and getting the information you need is a dance that you might mess up the steps to at first, but you will get the hang of it the more you practice!

Chapter Seven

There Is (Almost Always) a Rhyme or a Reason to It

One of the biggest challenges to being a junior Biglaw associate is the lack of control you will have over your schedule. Luckily, there are ways to add some control back into your life (we'll delve more into that in *Chapters Nineteen* and *Twenty*, which are all about finding balance and making Biglaw work for you). Even so, being at the bottom of the Biglaw food chain means there will be plenty of things that you can't control. Many of your assignments won't make any sense to you, but I promise you, there is almost always a rhyme or a reason for the request. Hopefully, this chapter will clear up some of the mystery around these seemingly random requests and better equip you to respond to them.

Here is a typical situation you might face:

Out of the blue, a partner sends you an email at 6:00 p.m. with an urgent task that you must complete before you leave for the evening. It's for a matter that's been dormant for three months that suddenly came back, without any warning. You had come to work early that morning to get your work done so you could leave by 7:00 p.m. to make it to your friend's birthday dinner. Looks like you'll be missing that dinner, so you send a quick text to your friend to let him know you won't be there.

Bummed out, you turn to the assignment and take however many hours you need to complete it before sending it off to the partner and heading home. Disappointed that you missed the dinner but satisfied that you were able to get your work done by the deadline and eager to hear the partner's feedback, your email will be met with silence.

You'll double-check your outbox to make sure the email was actually sent (it was). Three more days will pass and you still won't have heard a peep. Finally, at 6:30 a.m. and an entire week after the urgent draft was due, you will receive a mark-up with comments for you to address. What happened between the urgent request and the time the partner finally got back to you? Could your urgent assignment have waited a few days? Did you have to miss your plans for this? Did he give you this arbitrary deadline just because he could?

Things That You Don't See Control Timing

Situations like the one I just described are common in Biglaw. When something like this first happens to you, it will drive you crazy. The following thoughts might run through your mind as you sit at your desk, trying to suppress the anger that is boiling up inside: I know I am just a junior associate, but how could he not respect my time, even a little bit? If he wasn't going to look at it for a week, how urgent was it, really?

These reactions are natural, but it is seldom the case that a senior associate or partner would give you a wholly arbitrary and unreasonable deadline just to make your life miserable. There is a rhyme or a reason to it. Let me try to convince you of this and give you some tips on how to figure out the reason behind a request so you don't let yourself spiral into a fit of rage.

Something More Urgent Came Up

That end of the day deadline? The partner had to give it to you because the client told him she needed it by noon the next day. The partner was planning to review your work the following morning, until he spoke with the client at 9:00 a.m. and something even more urgent came up, and the partner and the client agreed to push back whatever it was you had worked on until this pressing issue was resolved. When it was resolved, and when the client asked again about your work, the partner picked it back up and finished his review, a week later than originally planned.

One thing Biglaw partners have mastered is triage. They must manage the urgency of their clients' demands and advise their clients as to what is most pressing. Your assignment simply got bumped down the list by another, more urgent matter, and the partner dealt with the timing behind the scenes. Sometimes you will be privy to this information and the reasoning behind the last-minute, adjusted timeline, but sometimes you won't be.

Partners Are Juggling a Lot

Another reason you might get a "fake" deadline is because of the sheer amount of work that a partner has on his plate and the various client demands he is constantly juggling. A great partner I worked for would often take a few days (by no means a long time) to review and provide feedback on something he asked me to draft. Expect that a partner or senior attorney will build in a buffer for when something is due and when he plans to review it. It's hard to know precisely when a partner will have time to review something, but when he does have time, the assignment better be drafted and ready for him to review. It was more efficient and easier for him, and for everyone who worked for him, to ask his associates to draft something a few days early than to have to wait on it.

If a senior attorney abuses her power and disrespects your time by giving you urgent and arbitrary deadlines over and over again, that's a different story. However, I found that the majority of the time, the senior attorney just had so much on her plate that she had to be ready to turn to anything at a moment's notice when a client asked for it. If she plans ahead, the partner can turn something around to a client without having to wait on a first-year associate to first "take a crack at it" (a code phrase in Biglaw for having a junior associate prepare a first draft that usually needs extensive rewriting).

How Can You Help Yourself?

There are a couple of things you can do to understand the rhyme or reason behind what you are asked to do.

Just Ask

When someone gives you an assignment, always ask when the deadline is. When the deadline is extremely short, it's perfectly fine to ask for more information to try to decipher why. Be careful how you question a deadline, but you can ask for more information, such as when will the work product be sent to the client, or what is going on with the deal that has caused this assignment to become so urgent (for example, did the partner just get an angry call from the client or is the client about to go on vacation and needs to see the work ASAP?). The worst that can happen is that you don't get an answer or any further information, and you go back to your desk and get the work done.

See the Big Picture and Keep It in Mind

Lots of tasks you'll receive as a junior associate will be discrete and will make up a very tiny piece of a larger puzzle. If you understand that larger puzzle, and not just your limited role in it, you will find yourself less confused and more in the loop when it comes to timing. It will be easier to understand why certain things are asked of you and why a deadline is what it is.

Aside from understanding why you are doing something, being able to see the big picture is central to your success in Biglaw. It's crucial to make the jump from junior associate to mid-level associate that you understand how what you are doing fits into the whole case or deal.

Client Events and Other Firm Things That Take Up a Partner's Time

Does it seem like the partners you work with are never in the office? That they are traveling to conferences or out to dinner at yet another fantastic restaurant, leaving you behind to deal with an ornery client? You might think to yourself, if the partner were around, your life would be so much easier *and* the client would get what he wants (an answer from the partner, not from you). On top of not being around, and having you suffer through the work alone, he is somewhere you'd rather be – eating delicious food and drinking fancy cocktails!

Leaving the junior associate behind to suffer while more senior attorneys go out and have fun might sound like a special kind of torture. It took some time for me to realize it, but there is a rhyme or a reason to this, too. A partner *has* to do these things. He has to go to dinner with a client, even if he doesn't particularly like that client and isn't interested in eating another heavy Italian dinner when he's on a diet. It turns out that once you get invited to a few of those client dinners, you realize they aren't all they're cracked up to be. Client development isn't always as glamorous or as fun as it looks from the outside. Understanding that it is part of the partner's job to participate in these client dinners and events should make you feel better when you're stuck back at the office, left to complete a task on your own. That, and the fact that your turn will come, too, and when it does, you'll understand.

~ ~ ~

Most of the time, there will be a rhyme or a reason for something that, at first glance, seems arbitrary or unnecessarily urgent. As a junior associate, you are there to serve the partners and the firm's clients. Sometimes that means completing an assignment at an inconvenient time for you but a convenient time for them. It might mean getting left behind at the office to work so others can do the client-facing part of the job. Whatever it is, it's part of being a Biglaw associate and the sooner you accept it as part of your job, the sooner you'll find peace amidst the chaos.

Chapter Eight

Making, Owning Up to, and Handling Mistakes

You will probably make mistakes every day. It is how you react to those mistakes and find solutions to the problems your mistakes may have created that matters. Problem solving is what lawyers do, after all, and a mistake is simply an additional small (or sometimes giant) bump in the road that needs to be smoothed over. A junior associate who views his mistakes as challenges to overcome and problems to solve, as opposed to something to be ashamed of or to hide, will be more successful than one who panics or tries to cover them up.

A Note on Perfectionism

If you are a perfectionist, which is extremely likely if you are a Biglaw lawyer, you will struggle in Biglaw unless you let some of that perfectionism go. The problem is, clients who pay extraordinary amounts of money for your work expect perfection. Even though clients and partners understand (at least in theory) that mistakes can happen, those same clients and partners do not expect mistakes to happen on *their* deals. Clients certainly do not pay hundreds or thousands of dollars an hour (yes – thousands – for certain partners) for your time for anything less than absolutely perfect work product. Likewise, partners do not want someone on their team who does not provide the perfect work product that clients expect.

But Biglaw lawyers are human, too, and make mistakes—all of the time. As a diligent associate, you should work hard, do your absolute best, and strive to make as few mistakes as possible. But mistakes will be made. You will stay up for days or even weeks at a time with little to no sleep and you will miss something. Pieces will be moving so fast that it will be impossible to keep up. Everything is so new that something will slip through the cracks. You must learn to drop the expectation of perfection you've placed on yourself, because it is a bar you will never meet. You can only be diligent and do your very best, and then fix the mistakes you make.

Your work doesn't have to be perfect per se, but everything you turn in must be "A" quality work and be done to the best of your ability. If you deliver anything less, you are not doing your job. I've heard the advice (not in the Biglaw arena) that it is better to put out "B-" work than no work at all. This advice might be accurate for an entrepreneur or an artist trying to get their work out into the world, but it is not true for a Biglaw associate. Your first draft can be "B-" quality, but before you turn it in to a senior attorney or a client, it better be revised and reflect your "A" game.

How to Handle a Mistake: Acknowledge the Mistake and Brainstorm Solutions

This chapter is not about how to prevent a mistake, but about what to do when you inevitably make one. No matter how small it is or how insignificant you think it may be, don't ignore the mistake and proceed as if you didn't notice it and hope that nobody else will. This tactic might work on a rare occasion, but in all likelihood, it will not. Even if it does work in the short-term, covering up a mistake will usually come back to bite you when you least expect it. Whether it is later on during the deal or many years later during litigation over the transaction, your mistake in all likelihood will be found. It is better to fix it now while you still can.

So what *should* you do when you realize you've messed something up? First, acknowledge the mistake and assess the situation. Before you go running to your supervisor to talk about it, pause for a moment or two and think about the error. Is it a simple one that you see an immediate fix for? If so, make the fix, but only if you are confident you've found the correct solution.

A word of caution here: a junior associate often thinks he has found the easy fix to a solution, so he makes the change. But, from experience, a more senior attorney would have known that, for one reason or another, something else must be done in order to fix the problem properly. Best practice is to run your solution by a senior associate first, detailing your mistake and your plan for fixing it. If he agrees with your proposed solution, go ahead and fix it. By checking in first, you will leverage the experience of the senior members of your team and you will be confident in your solution the next time a similar issue arises and will be able to solve it alone.

When you assess the scope of your mistake and decide you need help to fix it, first, make sure you fully understand the issue and what happened. Then, come up with a way to explain the issue clearly to the senior person on your team with whom you plan to raise the issue. Since he probably was not as intimately involved with this particular aspect of the transaction as you were, you will have to explain it to him. Next, come up with one or more proposed solutions to fix the problem. When you have all of that information organized, present the facts, the problem, and your possible solutions to him in a calm manner. It's important not to go running to him like a maniac, rambling incoherently about missing signature pages or comments that were never included in a document but should have been.

No matter how big the mistake, by approaching it professionally and proposing a solution, you will have done your job. I can't promise you won't get yelled at (although this is rare) or scolded for messing up, but I can promise you that the majority of the time you will sit down with whatever senior attorney on the team you are working with and the two of you will fix the issue together. It might involve an uncomfortable call to a client, a late night spent at the office reworking a document, or an upset opposing counsel, but in the end, you will handle it, and you will all move on. Remember that hardly anything you can do is career-ending, unfixable, or *that* bad, especially if you're otherwise a diligent associate.

Nobody Knows Everything and Everyone Makes Mistakes

Guess what? Nobody in Biglaw, not even the most experienced and senior partner, knows everything and everybody, at every level, makes mistakes because nobody is perfect.

(A brief caveat here: just because everyone makes mistakes, doesn't mean that all mistakes will be forgiven. If you consistently make the same mistakes or make mistakes out of laziness or because you don't care about the assignment, no matter how well you fix those mistakes, this will be frowned upon and rightfully so.)

If you don't know everything, it means you are human, just like the rest of us, and that you'll make mistakes, too. When I was a first-year associate, I was working one-on-one with an attorney who had just made partner. When we met in October during my first week of work, he was technically still an associate. By the time January rolled around, he had moved to a bigger office and had officially become a partner.

That winter, a complicated issue came up on our deal. As we sat in his office brainstorming what to do, I waited for him to come up with the answer since he was the partner after all. Surely he would know. Then, he surprised me by saying, "Let's call Bill to ask what he thinks because I'm not sure which approach to take." I was shocked that he would have to call Bill, a senior partner in our group, to ask for advice. He was a partner; didn't that mean he knew the answer to everything?

Looking back on this, it was crazy for me to think that just because he was a partner, that meant that he would know the answer to everything. Like me, he was still learning. In fact, even the more senior partners I ended up working for later in my career constantly reached out to other partners and even associates for advice and guidance. Whether the issue is new to them, out of their area of expertise, or just something they want a second opinion on, Biglaw lawyers are continually learning and asking each other for help, because nobody knows everything.

(As an aside, this also highlights one of the most amazing things about working in Biglaw. There are more available resources, which include the minds of other lawyers, at your disposal than you will find at most other offices. You're lucky to work in Biglaw with the chance to work with and learn from these people.)

Back to those mistakes. Can you really recover from them, even the bad ones, and succeed in Biglaw, one day even making partner? Definitely. A partner I worked for used to keep a copy of an offering circular (for those of you not in Capital Markets, these are 200- or 300-page documents detailing the terms of an offering that investors receive) that he had worked on as a mid-level associate on a shelf in his office. It was common for attorneys to keep copies of past deals they worked on to use as references for future, similar deals, or just to have as a record of what they had accomplished.

Early on in my career, I made a mistake that I had to go to this partner to discuss. I was stressed about it, but I owned up to my error and approached him with a possible solution. We called the client together and fixed the issue. After the call, he took one of the many offering circulars down off of his shelf and asked me to flip to the back of the document where the financial tables were attached. He explained that he kept this offering circular, from a non-descript, not-so-special deal from fifteen years prior, for just one reason. He had been in charge of compiling the sections of the offering circular and signing off on the whole thing before it was printed and distributed to investors, and he had accidentally included the wrong financial statements.

Now, other people had reviewed the draft and had signed off

on the book for printing, too, but it was ultimately his responsibility to make sure the correct financial statements were included. This printed offering circular went out to the various investors on the deal, the firm's corporate client, and the other side and their counsel. Needless to say, this was more than just a small mistake. Once an investor pointed out that they had been given incorrect information, the book had to be reprinted with the correct financial statements, the firm's client had to tell all of the other investors about the mistake (which was embarrassing) and new, corrected, books had to be printed and re-distributed.

But guess what? Nothing terrible happened. My boss owned up to his mistake, worked to fix it, and (after many more mistakes, I'm sure, and lots of hard work) he became a partner. He works on similar transactions with that same client to this day.

~ ~ ~

Ultimately, none of us know everything (especially as a new associate) and mistakes are bound to happen. No matter how big or small the mistake, it is how you own up to it and fix it that makes all the difference.

Chapter Nine

Asking for, Implementing, and Giving Feedback

Consistent and quality feedback is one of the key things you need to advance in Biglaw and become a successful junior associate. So important, in fact, that it can make the difference between a successful associate and one who lasts just a few years and fizzles out.

Why is feedback so valuable as a junior associate? As a new lawyer, you often don't know what you're doing wrong and what you're doing right unless you are directly told one way or the other. Things move quickly in Biglaw and multiple layers of attorneys often review your work. You might turn in an assignment to a fourth-year associate who reviews it, makes changes, and sends it to a partner who makes additional changes before sending it to a client. Depending on your relationship with the other members of the team and with the client, you may or may not be copied on that final email to the client. If you aren't, and if nobody reaches out to you with feedback, there will be no way of knowing how good (or bad) your draft was. If it was great, it would be nice to know what about it was great, so that you can repeat that. If it was terrible, it would be even better to know what was so terrible about it, so that you know never to repeat that. Without feedback on your work, you remain in the dark as to how you are doing.

You might think that whether or not you receive feedback is out of your control since it will be up to the senior attorney to give it to you, after all, but this is not true. There are plenty of ways you can help yourself get the quality feedback you need to grow and plenty of things you should do with the feedback you do get. There is also a time and place for you to give feedback to others. Let's delve into all things feedback-related now.

Getting Feedback: Sometimes You Have to Ask for It

Some attorneys are great at giving feedback. They will sit with you and explain in-depth what you did well and what you can improve on for the next time. You may also receive indirect feedback when you get your draft work back from them with comments to address and incorporate into the next draft. This is not direct feedback (meaning, the lawyer does not sit down with you one-on-one to discuss his comments), but receiving a mark-up of your work is a form of feedback because you can see for yourself what changes were made. After some time, you'll come to better understand what the changes mean and whether or not you provided a quality draft.

Other attorneys will not give you any feedback. You will turn in a draft and never hear back from them, leaving you to wonder whether your work was perfect, total trash, or something in between.

No matter how good a senior lawyer is at giving feedback, everyone gets busy and feedback is one of the first things to fall by the wayside during hectic times. For this reason, you must develop the habit of asking for feedback, regularly. If you have some downtime, schedule a few minutes with a senior lawyer and ask if he can give you feedback on your recent work. Make it easy for him by giving him the heads-up and asking for feedback on specific assignments, not just for general feedback, as it might be hard for him to come up with valuable content for you on the spot.

Let's say you recently drafted twenty-five closing documents for a corporate reorganization and the senior associate marked them up and shared his comments with you, but never actually discussed what his comments meant. It is very important to know the difference between stylistic changes, things he wouldn't have expected you to know as a junior associate, and comments he made because you were sloppy or you misunderstood something you should have known. Unless you ask, you'll never know which bucket his comments fell into. He might be stewing in his office thinking about how bad a job you did and telling other associates all about it, which is something you want to nip in the bud. Or you might have done a relatively good job. Either way, there's something to learn.

A great time to ask for feedback is when a deal, project, or case ends. A comprehensive break-down session to review what went well and what could be improved upon for next time can be extremely valuable. Quality senior associates will want your feedback as well, so take advantage of this opportunity to voice your opinions. Ultimately, almost every senior associate will be appreciative that you took the time to ask him for feedback so that the next time you turn in an assignment to him, you won't make the same mistakes and your work product will be improved. This brings us to the most important part of feedback: implementing it.

Implementing Feedback

The best feedback in the world won't mean anything unless you do something with it. There's really not much to it: take in whatever feedback you are given and then make a real effort to show that you took the feedback seriously by implementing it.

Were you told that you were making too many sloppy mistakes? That you need to tell the senior attorney when you will be unavailable in the evenings? That your tone when speaking with a client needs to change? Whatever the feedback was, the next time you work with the attorney who gave you the feedback, be extra careful to take her advice and correct whatever it was that she asked you to improve.

Asking for feedback and then *not* implementing it is worse than never asking at all. Senior attorneys will wonder why they took the time to teach you something if you are going to ignore it, so be conscious of this and take what they say seriously and act on it.

What to Do With Negative Feedback

Even the best junior associates don't receive gold stars and positive feedback all of the time. You will get some negative feedback from time to time, and you must tough it out. Have confidence in yourself and your skills even when the approval you're seeking isn't there or the feedback isn't so great. Some negative feedback will be legitimate. From it, you'll learn what changes to make, and you will move on, having grown from the experience. Other times, you will work with someone you just don't mesh well with, and that's OK, too. It takes some trial and error to find the people in Biglaw who you work best with.

When I was a first-year associate, I was staffed on two intense deals at the same time with two different partners. Each was staffed leanly, so it was just me, another associate, and the partner, and I was struggling on both deals. I didn't feel like I was giving either of the deals the attention it deserved, and something just wasn't clicking with me on either deal for one reason or the other, even though I was working my tail off.

Sometimes that happens, and sometimes you will receive negative feedback. That's what happened to me. The partners each met with me and asked me if I cared about the deals or the work. During those meetings, I wanted to crawl into a hole and disappear. I promised them I would try harder (although at the time I had no idea how I could possibly try harder). I imagine the group I ended up working with for the next six years would have been shocked if they knew my work ethic was ever questioned. I received negative feedback that stung, but I also got another shot to find my way by working with people with whom I got along much better. If something similar happens to you, make sure to take that second chance and keep going.

What If You Can't Get Any Feedback?

What happens if your requests for feedback go unanswered? Sometimes you just aren't going to get any feedback, either negative or positive, until your annual review. Even then, the feedback will be boiled down into a somewhat meaningless summary and will be conveyed to you by whatever partner gives the reviews (usually the head of the group and someone you never work with).

If this is the only feedback you can get, it is not ideal, but there is only so much you can do about it because you can't *force* anyone to give you guidance if they don't want to. If you find yourself in this situation and are wondering if you are doing well or not, you can try talking to someone in associate development. Firms usually have someone (or even a whole group of people) devoted to associate development. While it's not nearly as helpful as talking to the attorneys you work with, they can be a resource for you if you are looking for guidance as to how you are doing. They can act as liaisons with the partners and put in a request for feedback on your behalf. At the very least, they can assure you that you're doing all right if you are worried.

Giving Feedback

You need to learn how to give quality feedback, too. Even as a first-year associate, you'll have the opportunity to mentor and provide feedback to paralegals and summer associates. By the time your first summer at the firm rolls around, you will have a few deals or projects under your belt, and you will be fully capable of giving quality feedback. The summer is an excellent time to hone your skills at giving feedback. Work with as many summer associates as possible and, after every assignment they turn in, sit down with them to review how they did. When the new first-year associates arrive at the firm a few months later, you will already be in the habit of giving feedback.

If you sharpen this skill early on in your career, you will be a major asset to the firm. Junior associates will want to work with you because they will know that they can expect to receive feedback from you. People love to know where they stand, especially in Biglaw, where junior associates often feel as though they never know if they're doing a good job or not. By providing feedback, you'll also help develop the junior associates into better lawyers, which is beneficial to everyone (yourself included) in the long run.

The chance to give upward feedback is not as common, so when the opportunity arises, take it. Some firms have formal processes where you can provide feedback on and rate the senior attorneys you work with. This upward feedback is usually anonymous, so it is a good way to share your opinions on senior attorneys openly. You might not otherwise ever get the chance. If nothing else, it's a cathartic experience to put your thoughts on record, anonymously.

~ ~ ~

Feedback is essential to your growth and ultimate success as an associate. Give the senior associates and partners you work with every opportunity to give you feedback. Constantly ask for it and then implement it. Hone your skills as a giver of feedback by first practicing with paralegals and summer associates so by the time you are a mid-level associate you will have developed the habit of giving constant feedback. Lastly, never miss the (somewhat rare) chance to provide upward feedback when presented with the opportunity.

Chapter Ten

Mastering the Art of Billing

The billable hour is Biglaw's most important metric. The more billable hours the firm's attorneys record, the more money the firm makes (for the most part; you'll see in this chapter why every hour billed does not necessarily equal an hour earned). All Biglaw lawyers are required to track their work by the hour (well, in six-minute increments, actually) and clients pay a specific hourly rate for each attorney. The more junior you are, the lower this hourly billing rate is, but that rate is still hundreds of dollars per hour worked. It can even reach a thousand dollars (or more) per hour for experienced partners.

At the end of a matter (or at designated intervals, if it is a long-term project), the partner will send a bill to the client listing every attorney who worked on the matter, each one's hourly rate, how many hours each spent working on it, and a narrative of what each attorney did during every one of those hours. The goal is to "collect on" (i.e., get paid for) every single hour an attorney billed to the client.

For various reasons, collecting on and getting paid for all of the work billed to a client doesn't always happen. For one, clients often push back on the amount of time attorneys spent on certain tasks or are surprised at the overall cost of the transaction, so partners end up negotiating the bill with them and agreeing to a lower amount. It has also become more common in Biglaw for partners to agree to a flat-fee up front. This means a partner will tell the client what the total cost of the project will be and, no matter how many hours are billed to it (either less than expected or more than expected), the agreed-upon fee is what the client ultimately pays. Associates will still enter their hours for purposes of the firm's recording system, but the client will not pay for every one of those hours like they would in the traditional hourly fee model.

Sometimes a partner will let you know if the matter is a flat-fee or hourly billed one, but for your purposes, it shouldn't make a difference. The information that follows on billing practices is applicable no matter what the final bill to the client turns out to be.

Now that the concept of the billable hour and why it is so important to the firm ($$$) is hopefully clear, let's dive into why the billable hour is so important to junior associates. These are some things you can and should do when it comes to billing practices so that you remain in good standing with your firm.

Your Time Entries

Your billable hours have to be reported to the firm and the client somehow. At the end of every day, every attorney is required to submit electronic "diary entries," which detail exactly how much time, down to 0.1 of an hour (six minutes), he spent and what exactly he did during that time.

We'll only touch upon this briefly, as every firm has its own policy that it will tell you about (or rather, beat into your head) during firm orientation. Generally speaking, you should know that firms take these time entries *very* seriously since billing and collecting on those bills is how they make their money. Some firms even punish associates financially (either by deducting amounts from their paycheck or docking their year-end bonus) for late or poorly written time entries. While the last thing you'll want to do at the end of an eighteen-hour day is enter your time, when you think about it, the firm's requirement that you do this every day makes sense. No time entries means no money for the firm. So take the time every day to enter your hours worked and a description of what you worked on.

Entering your time benefits you, too, and not just because it helps you escape punishment. Supposedly, if you record your time late (e.g., waiting until the end of the week to enter the entire week's worth of time and trying to remember what you did every hour of that week, by combing through emails, calendar appointments, etc.), you will actually *underestimate* the number of hours you worked. You not only cheat the firm of time worked, but you cheat yourself, too. Hopefully, this, combined with the prospect of losing some of your compensation, is enough to incentivize you to get your time entries done on time. It really is in your best interest to input your time, every single day.

Hitting Your Target Billable Hours

To remain in good standing with the firm, which means you get to keep your job and hopefully receive a generous year-end bonus, all associates must work at least the minimum number of hours the firm expects of them. While it is up to others (whether it is a senior associate, partner, or a designated staffing department) to staff junior associates on assignments, each associate is ultimately responsible for working enough throughout the year to work this minimum number of hours, otherwise known as "hitting" or "making" your target billable hours.

Your firm's policy on its hours' expectations will be made very clear to you on your first day of work (if you don't already know it from doing your own research ahead of time). It is standard policy in the Biglaw world for associates to work 2,000 hours per year. If you don't, you risk being let go or, at the very least, not getting your bonus. Depending on your firm, the hours' requirement could be a little less or a little more, but most will be right around that 2,000-hour mark.

This is not 2,000 hours of time spent in the office. It's 2,000 hours of recorded, chargeable (to a client or the firm) hours. This is what that means: of those 2,000 hours, many firms allow a certain number (200 is pretty standard) to consist of non-billable (non-client) work and still count toward the 2,000-hour requirement. Non-billable hours are usually limited to things like pro bono, time devoted to firm committees, or time spent researching and writing a legal paper. You should review the details of your firm's policy so you know exactly what counts and what doesn't toward your target number.

Now that you understand how many hours you should strive for during a year, how can you hit those hours? The best (and easiest) way to make your hours is to do great work. By doing great work, not only do you develop your legal skills, but people will want to work with you more. Senior attorneys will staff you on their projects over and over again because you have proven to be a valuable asset. The hours will naturally come. Not only will you have an easy time making your hours, but you will also end up with the most interesting and best work those attorneys have to offer, so it's a win-win.

What to Do When You Are Struggling to Get Hours

Sometimes even doing great work won't guarantee that you'll have enough of it. At times, you might not be very busy. That's acceptable for a while, but if you consistently bill very few hours or are not getting work but others at your level are, it's time to take action. If you are concerned about your lack of work, there are a few things you can do about it:

- Talk to someone, either a partner in the group in charge of staffing or the staffing department, about it. You might have slipped through the cracks, there might not be that much work to go around, or there could be concerns about your work. These are all things you'd want to know and might not be told unless you ask.
- Ask around to anyone in your group, on your floor, or who you've heard might need some help, if they have work available. Be proactive and look for work outside of the normal assignment system and outside of the people you regularly work with.
- Don't be afraid to have "too much" work sometimes. Hours in Biglaw ebb and flow, so there will be times you have too much work that you have to balance with down-time. During a down-time, continue asking multiple attorneys for work, even if you're afraid they will all say yes and you will be

staffed on multiple things. You will figure it out and manage to get it all done.

If you are struggling to reach your required billable hours because of things outside of your control, such as a downturn in the economy, there are other things you can do to keep busy. When I was a first-year associate, the economy was still recovering from the financial crisis of 2008 and work was not as abundant as it had been in prior years. Before my class of associates even arrived that fall, my firm had laid off many associates.

There was no way associates in certain groups were going to be able to hit 2,000 billable hours that year. They essentially had the choice to either work a low number of billable hours and nothing more or use their extra time to do something productive for the firm. Many chose the first option, but the ones who stood out chose the second one. While I was lucky enough to be in a group that had sufficient work, a colleague in the litigation group was not. Instead of going home early or idling all day like some of his classmates, he chose to spend hours and hours (probably at least 1,000) working on a pro bono project he was passionate about. Guess who definitely was not laid off at the end of that year? That guy. Biglaw might value the billable hour above all else, but when there is not enough billable work to go around, pro bono is a valuable way to gain skills and show the firm you are devoted to your work and eager to learn.

Check in on Where You Stand Early and Often

Your firm's billing software will make it extremely easy to know at all times where you stand and whether or not you are on pace to hit your hours by the end of the year. Use this to check in on yourself early and often. If you are way above pace, and anticipate the work to continue at the same rate for the rest of the year, take this as an opportunity to take a vacation.

On the other hand, if you are way below where you should be, if you realize this early on in the year, you will have plenty of time to catch up. What you *shouldn't* do is wait until Thanksgiving to check on your hours and see that you need more work and you need it soon. Getting work around the holidays can be unpredictable. You might get "lucky" and get staffed on a crazy matter that needs to close by the end of the year, but you might not. It always smells fishy when junior associates desperately start asking for work around this time, especially if they haven't done so all year. If an associate were to come by looking for work in July, nobody would think twice about staffing him, but that all changes at the end of the year when you know he's just looking to make his hours. Plan ahead, by tracking your time over the course of the year, and people will be happy to staff you appropriately.

Hit Your Hours, but Never Over-Bill

Your firm can only get paid for the hours you bill if the client is willing to pay for those hours. If a client refuses to pay for work you have billed, the partner has to "write off" that time and the firm's bottom line takes a hit. A client refusing to pay for your work is not usually your fault (in fact, even written off hours count toward your yearly hours goal), but you should be cognizant of how much you bill. Clients will scrutinize the bill and refuse to pay if they don't think the firm provided value equal to what it's charging.

It can be difficult as a junior associate to know if you are spending the appropriate amount of time on a task. While nobody expects you to perform your work at record speed, you should follow some general parameters when it comes to how long a task takes. First, always ask the senior associate or partner how long they expect the particular assignment to take. They'll give you an estimate and if you don't expect to be done within that time frame, check in with them to let them know your progress. The partner will probably realize that he underestimated the time he thought it would take and tell you to take another X amount of hours to finish up. It is always better to ask for permission ahead of time than to ask for forgiveness for over-billing.

When you ask how long an assignment should take, you may hear a common Biglaw refrain: it should take as long as it takes. This is meant to assure associates that so long as they focus on the work and provide good quality work product, it does not matter how many hours they bill. This sentiment, however, is left over from the old days of Biglaw, when (so I hear) you could invoice a client any amount and they would pay it without batting an eye. If you are told this, try to press for an estimate so you have a ballpark range to shoot for. Clients today are not so willing to pay for what they deem to be wasteful.

If you do grossly overbill on an assignment, you might not be told that you did anything wrong (even if the partner had to write off your time). You simply won't be staffed again by that associate or that group because it is part of your job to be efficient. That's why you should always ask for a time estimate at the beginning of a new assignment.

Another way associates over-bill is by doing work that is beneath them. As you advance in your career, you will be expected to take on new challenges and leave certain tasks behind for the new crop of junior associates to tackle. Some mid-level associates make the mistake of continuing to do work better suited for junior associates or even paralegals. In a pinch, every attorney, even partners, find themselves doing work a first-year associate could complete, but this should be the exception, not the norm. A third-year associate should no longer spend ten hours organizing signature pages the night before a closing. A first-year associate should do that, both so the first-year associate learns how to do it and because a client does not want to pay for a third-year associate to do that work. By that point, they are simply too expensive for certain tasks. A third-year associate who bills 2,000 hours a year, but 1,000 of those hours could have and should have been completed by a first-year associate, is not doing anyone any favors. She is neither progressing nor providing value to the firm, as the client will likely refuse to pay for some of her time.

Why It's Important to Understand the Bill

It falls on the partner to send the final bill to a client so that he can get paid for his team's work. A junior associate might never see the bill, but should keep his eyes and ears open for any discussion about it. Some partners talk openly about their bills or ask their associates to help prepare them, while others are more private about them.

If you plan to stay in Biglaw long-term, understanding the bill and the nuances of negotiating it with clients will be an essential skill to your success. Even if you do not plan on a long-term career, knowing what goes into a bill is still helpful. For example, you might be told outright or get a sense from the senior attorneys on the matter that the bill is tight (meaning the team has already billed many hours to the deal, the client was not expecting it to be so expensive, and there's still work to be done). In this case, it is even more important than usual to be efficient and mindful of how many hours you bill.

The bill can also show you:

- What type of work the partner agrees to write off.
- What a partner is willing to negotiate ahead of time, in terms of pricing.
- How much pressure clients put on partners to cut the bill.
- What type of work clients are willing to pay for (generally, they will pay almost anything for work that requires highly skilled experts; on the other hand, they will fight tooth and nail over a high bill for a routine matter that almost any lawyer could complete).

~ ~ ~

The billable hour is the most valuable metric the firm has to assess your performance. You are in charge of making sure you get sufficient work to hit your hours so you can stay on track, remain in good standing with the firm, and receive your bonus. Doing good work goes a long way toward getting enough work, but sometimes you have to be proactive and seek out the work or fill up your time doing something else for the firm to keep yourself busy.

Be cognizant of how much you are billing and keep your ears open for expectations as to time management. If you work efficiently, enter your time correctly, and do good work, you'll have mastered the art of billing and will be right where you should be.

Chapter Eleven

Using Technology and Email to Your Advantage

When used correctly, technology and email can save you an enormous amount of time and help you produce your best quality work. There are some pitfalls to watch out for, but for the most part, the better you understand and use technology and email, the easier your Biglaw life will be.

Mastering Technology

Technology is an area of Biglaw where you, as a brand-new junior associate, will have the advantage over many other attorneys in your office. The difference between the generations of senior attorneys who grew up without most modern technology (iPhones, laptops, fancy office phones, etc.) and your generation, who did grow up with these things, is most apparent when it comes to mastering, understanding, and using technology to your advantage. The younger you are, the more likely the better you will be at grasping new technology, while many of the more senior people you work with will not be quite as tech-savvy.

Aside from saving yourself time and helping you produce higher-quality work, understanding the firm's technology inside and out means you will be an asset to your team in potentially stressful situations. Without a doubt, there will come a time when you are gathered in a partner's office waiting for a conference call to begin and nobody can figure out how to join the call or connect the video. If you can calmly walk over to the phone, computer, or whatever other gadget you're dialing in from and fix the problem before the call starts, you will have just provided value. It might not seem all that important, but it is often the little things in Biglaw that are remembered, and this is no exception. Junior associates might not be valued (yet) for their brilliant legal minds, but showing your value in any way counts.

Become an Expert on the Basics and on Firm-Specific Tools

If you aren't already an expert on the basic programs that you'll be using every day, such as Word, Excel, PowerPoint, and other Microsoft Office programs, become one. Ask a friend at the firm who is tech-savvy to spend an afternoon with you teaching you whatever you need to learn to get up to speed.

When you join the firm, you will sit through hours of new-associate orientation sessions. Pay close attention to the technology-specific sessions that review firm-specific tools. Take the time to learn how to use every single piece of technology you might use in your day-to-day work, from the printers to the phones (like how to join, merge, and forward calls and how to put someone on hold), to video conference technology, to the conference room speaker system, and so on. If there's anything you don't understand after a brief introduction and a little practice back in your office, when in doubt, ask for help.

Ask the Firm's IT Department for Help

Many firms outsource much of their IT issues to hubs in lower-cost countries. Instead of having a team on-site, most of the technology staff will be accessible only via a phone call. While having someone in your office to fix your problem might be easier, it's just not cost-efficient. Calling the help desk can and often does resolve your minor issues, but if you can become self-sufficient, that's even better.

For those of us who are not naturally adept at picking up on new technology (raising my hand here), the firm's on-site technology department is an incredible resource. But wait, isn't the remote help-desk where you'll go for most of your tech issues? Yes, but there will still be an on-site IT group who can help, too (they just won't be available as immediately as the help-desk) and you can become self-sufficient by reaching out and learning from them.

The on-site team will be available to teach you how to use and take full advantage of all of the firm's resources. They can cater the tools they teach you how to use based on your practice area and your level of expertise. I found that whenever I reached out to the IT team, they loved to share their knowledge. At my firm, they were available to come to anyone's office to give personal tutoring sessions on how to use a particular application or program, to give presentations to your team about an issue that everyone was facing, or simply to answer a list of questions. If you need help or guidance on anything, schedule the time for one-on-one tech tutoring.

Technology Gives You Back Time and Flexibility

Being a master of technology will save you time and give you more flexibility. By knowing how to fix simple tech issues on your own, you'll be able to move on to the more essential things (your legal work). There's nothing worse than trying to get to work and encountering a technology roadblock that prevents you from doing so. When a temperamental printer acts up on a Friday evening after all the support staff have left for the weekend and you need to get original documents in the mail ASAP, knowing how to fix the ink cartridge yourself will save you both time and stress.

Not only will being good with technology help you when you are in the office, but those who can fix their own tech problems are also better at working from home. When it comes to working from home, "better" means being able to work as seamlessly as possible and creating as close to an in-office experience for your colleagues as possible (see *Chapter Seventeen* for more tips on how to accomplish this). Technology plays a huge role in making this work. For example, a first-year associate who is working from home but can't figure out how to connect to his office phone line is not much use to his senior team members on a day where they expect him to be available for client calls or to set up video conferences.

To create an optimal in-office and work-from-home experience for yourself, you have to ask for the resources that you need. Your firm will give you the basics, but if you need extras, like a hands-free headset for your conference calls or an extra laptop battery to keep at home, ask for them. You won't always get what you need, but it doesn't hurt to ask. If being able to work remotely is important to you, it's also worth it to invest your own money in extras, like a printer or a second monitor, that your firm won't necessarily give you but that will make your workspace more efficient. Just remember to run any potential purchase by your IT department before buying anything to make sure whatever you plan to get is compatible with the firm's equipment.

Email Best Practices

An entire book could be written about what not to do over email. You've probably heard of the most common email pitfalls, such as replying-all to a firm-wide email or sending an email directly to a client you're talking badly about instead of to your coworker. If you haven't already, there are some outrageous and true stories that you can find online on sites like *Above the Law* that can show you what not to do as an associate (e.g., don't brag in an email about how much money the firm spends on wining and dining you and how little you work, and then send that email to the entire firm).

These are the two basic pieces of advice you'll find almost everywhere:

1. Pretend as if every email you write will be made public or will be published on the front page of the New York Times.

2. What comes across one way in conversation may come across very differently over email, so be careful with your tone and, in particular, with any jokes.

If you follow these rules, they say, you won't run into trouble, and I agree with that. But we want to do more than avoid trouble – we want to make you an all-star junior associate. Here are a few pointers that you probably haven't already heard a million times before, but that will serve you well over your Biglaw career and get you on the right track. You'll pick up many more as you spend time in Biglaw, but these rules are a good addition to those and to the ones above.

Email Hierarchy

In Biglaw, hierarchy is so important (remember *Chapter One*?) that it even applies to how you address an email. When sending an email in Biglaw, you always list the recipients in descending order of seniority. For example, if you are sending an email to a client at a bank (and it's not addressed to just one person), you would list out their names in the "to" line in the following order: Managing Director, Director 1, Director 2, VP, Associate, Summer Intern; and list out your own colleagues' names in the "cc" line in the following order: Partner (if there is more than one, the most senior partner or the lead partner on the deal comes first and the others follow), Associates (ordered by seniority), and Paralegals. It's a minor detail, but it matters, so respect the rule and respect the hierarchy.

Email at the Appropriate Time

Just because you can send an email at any hour of the day doesn't mean that you should. If you are working on a non-urgent matter over the weekend, perhaps spare your recipient and wait to send it until Sunday evening or first thing on Monday morning. If you do want to send the email (maybe your team doesn't mind constant emails or *does* like to get things done on the weekend), include a note indicating that the question or the email is not urgent. No matter who you are dealing with (be it your own team, a client, or even a junior associate at another law firm), when sending things out during non-traditional business hours, it's always courteous to be clear about when you expect a response.

Emailing at appropriate times can help you, too. When you send something out, it usually means you will get something back. If you send something that is going to start a flurry of questions and back and forth, but you aren't prepared to answer those, wait until a better time. It's all about judgment, as with many things in Biglaw. Be courteous of others and protect your own interests. Email is an amazing tool, but it can also chain you to your desk (be it real or virtual) if it's not kept in check.

Red Flags

You know those red exclamation points that you can use in Microsoft Office to alert recipients that your email has arrived and that it is *very* important? Don't use this feature unless whatever you are sending is truly urgent (e.g., the deadline for closing a deal or submitting a court document is in fifteen minutes and you haven't received the required signature pages via email yet).

Your recipients will be on high-alert when they see that red flag. Most of the time, when I received an email with one of those red flags, it was not an emergency. Lawyers and their clients are already among the most stressed-out and on-edge group of people you'll come across, so don't make them even more so by ringing a false alarm. If you really do need an answer urgently, by all means, use the red flag, especially if you need to get the message out to a large group of people, but if you need to get the attention of one person or a small group, there's an even better option: the phone.

Use the Phone

As much as many junior associates hate to hear this, when something is urgent and needs to be resolved ASAP, the good old telephone is the way to go. As uncomfortable as it might be (nobody likes interrupting a high-strung client with an emergency phone call, but hiding behind an email is not the way to gain his trust or confidence), pick up the phone, make the call, and resolve the urgent issue.

Using the phone shouldn't be left just for emergencies. While email is great and is often the most efficient way to communicate with more than one person or to get complex ideas and questions onto paper so your recipient can thoughtfully review and have time to respond, a phone call can often resolve issues and answer questions much faster and more efficiently than an email ever can. Get into the habit as a junior associate of using the phone and I promise, once you get over any initial hesitation or anxiety, that you'll find it can be the most efficient way to communicate.

~ ~ ~

Technology and email will be an integral part of your everyday life in Biglaw, whether you are working at the office or at home. By mastering your firm's technology and learning best practices for email, you will set yourself up for success both at the office and while working remotely.

Chapter Twelve

Playing the Biglaw Game

There is so much more to Biglaw than billable client work. There is also so much more to becoming an outstanding associate than producing excellent work product. In addition to providing excellent legal work, to succeed in Biglaw, associates must also participate in all aspects of Biglaw firm life. Whether a client event, a firm cocktail hour, or a group volunteer project, this non-billable time is an essential part of Biglaw. Those who succeed in Biglaw, who enjoy it, and who have the best chance of a successful long-term career at a firm, understand that Biglaw is a game, they play the game, and they are good at the game. Here's how you can learn how to play that game, too.

Client Development

Landing your own clients and building a book of business is much buzzed about in the legal world. If you are interested in the ins-and-outs of business development, there are plenty of resources out there that detail how to market yourself and get clients. This book stops short of discussing business development directly, but it is tied to the lessons you'll learn here. No matter how great at marketing you become, if you don't have solid, foundational skills, you won't be able to keep any clients you do land. Master the skills in this book first and *then* worry about getting business.

Do you really need to have your own clients and book of business to succeed in Biglaw? The answer – absolutely not – might surprise you. Even if your goal is partnership, it is a misconception that an associate has to have her own clients and a full book of business by the time she makes partner. Instead, what usually happens is that the more senior partners you work with will have too much work on their plate and will share their work with you. You start as a junior partner on the deal and don't get credit with originating the work (i.e., you get paid less), but eventually, the clients become yours, too. (This is a story for another book, however. Back to client development for you, the junior associate.)

If you don't need a book of business, either because you don't plan on staying in Biglaw or because you believe what I just wrote, that doesn't mean that client development isn't necessary for all junior associates. Client events often include fun-sounding things like cocktail parties and four-course dinners complete with wine pairings. These things can be enjoyable, but the primary role an associate plays at these events is to make sure the clients have a good time. Client development is a non-billable firm activity that, while not mandatory, might as well be. These events don't happen that often, so you should make every effort to attend them to show the partner hosting the event for his clients that you are invested in your job. While associates aren't directly responsible for bringing in work, you are there to support the partners whose job *is* to bring in work. That the work keeps coming in is to your benefit, too, and this is a way to do your part to make sure that happens.

In addition to client events where you meet with clients in a more relaxed and informal environment, you will interact with clients every day and you should strive to make real, personal connections with them. It's unlikely (although not unheard of) for a junior associate to communicate directly with a company's general counsel or a bank's executive director, but you will be speaking and working directly with someone who works for those people.

And guess where today's assistant general counsel and junior banker are going to be in five or ten years? They will rise up the ranks at their respective jobs just as you will at your firm. One day, they will be the decision makers and in charge of hiring outside law firms. Working closely with someone when you are both in junior positions and getting to know that person on a personal level over time is one of the easiest ways to build your book of business, without ever having to go out and search for it.

Internal Firm Events

In addition to client events, your firm will host internal events. You'll have to attend these, too, but you don't have to go to all of them. From weekly group happy hours to lunchtime talks with guest speakers, there will be endless opportunities to attend events and network within your firm. As a junior associate, if you have the time, start by attending everything. Then, as you get a feel for what these events are all about, weed out the ones you don't enjoy and skip those.

Firm events are great places to bond with your colleagues. Whether it is a conference where you spend a few days with your fellow associates or a group retreat for the weekend, it is worth it to attend these to get to know your colleagues on a deeper level. One reason some Biglaw teams produce such great work is that they know each other so well. The better you know a colleague, the better your work often is.

Lastly, there's one more type of firm event: the annual holiday party and summer gala, which can be extravagant affairs, depending on your firm. You should always, always attend, and not because it is a "good place to network" or because you are expected to go, but because they can be truly enjoyable parties! It's nice to let loose once in a while with your coworkers, many of whom will become your true friends, all on the firm's dime.

Recruiting

One of the best ways to get involved with your firm as a junior associate is through recruiting for the next year's summer associate class during OCI. While you won't interview anyone just yet, junior associates are integral to the recruiting process. Volunteer to go to your law school for the day to answer questions from potential recruits or take students out to lunch or drinks after their interviews. Junior associates are there to offer law students a comfortable way to gain insight into the firm and are essential to recruiting the next class of quality associates.

Junior associates also continue the recruiting process when summer associates begin working at the firm. During the summer, the firm is still courting these students, trying to show them a good time and give them a good work experience so that they accept their offers to become full-time associates upon graduation. Junior associates are key members of this recruitment process. You will work directly with the summer associates and have the most time (and energy, probably!) to attend the many summer associate events. There, you will get to know the summer associates and give them the opportunity to get to know the firm better through you.

If you are active in recruiting during the OCI process and the summer, you will have fun and your participation will not go unnoticed. The recruiting team is usually very close with many of the firm's partners and they definitely talk to each other. Your hard work during recruiting and cultivating the next class of associates will eventually become known and appreciated.

Get to Know the Right People

Your long-term success in Biglaw will be aided by knowing the right people, which requires a bit of social and political maneuvering. If you do great work but nobody knows who you are aside from the few people you work with, you will do fine in Biglaw. If you really want to stand out, you need to branch out and get to know the right people.

How do you get to know some of these high-powered people at the firm, especially if none of them do the actual legal work that you are interested in? There are countless non-billable activities, such as committees and volunteer projects, that you can join. By working on a firm committee, for example, you might get to know a partner on the executive committee of the firm who doesn't usually interact with associates. Maybe the firm sponsors a yearly charity event that is the pet project of a powerful litigation partner. By participating in his volunteer project, you'll get to know him in a more relaxed environment.

Getting to know these partners might not help you in the short-term, but it could bring you into higher standing at the firm and you never know how that will pay off. This isn't about finding people and using them. You will put a lot of work into these extra-curricular activities and you should only participate in ones that you have a genuine interest in. There is nothing wrong with being strategic about your career and the choices you make. Having friends in high places never hurts, and it may come in handy in the future, whether it is for a reference or when you are up for partnership.

Keep your eyes and ears open to non-billable opportunities that make the most sense for your ultimate goals. Doing so might sound disingenuous to you, but it's all part of the Biglaw game. And if making partner is one of your goals, participating fully in firm life and playing the game is necessary. There's nothing that a Biglaw partner likes more than being a Biglaw partner. Letting a person into their exclusive club who does not feel the same way about their job and their firm is unlikely to happen.

~ ~ ~

You only have so many hours in a day and so much of yourself that you can devote to Biglaw, but don't forget the importance of fitting non-billable work into that time. Are you starting to understand why the 2,000-hour requirement doesn't mean you will be spending 2,000 hours per year in the office? This time might not all count toward those 2,000 hours, but it still counts. Whether it is spending time with your clients, your coworkers, law students, or others at the firm, non-billable hours can make the difference between a career that's a bust and one that's fulfilling and a success.

Chapter Thirteen

Finding Work That Is Interesting to You and That Motivates You

As you settle into your Biglaw career, the most crucial question to continuously ask yourself is whether or not you are genuinely interested in and like the work that you do. Unless that answer is an enthusiastic "Yes!," you may begin to struggle and feel like you're swimming against the current. You put yourself at a disadvantage if you don't like your work. Biglaw requires so much of its associates and it is much harder to give your all when you aren't interested. If the associate next to you is enthralled by the securities code and you could not care less, guess who is going to be more successful? Only by finding an area of the law that interests you, and finding what motivates you, will you set yourself up for success. Here's how you can begin to investigate what work fits the bill.

Are You Interested in Your Practice Area?

Law school classes might teach you how to "think like a lawyer," but they don't teach you how to be an excellent Biglaw associate (which is why you are reading this book!). Luckily, Biglaw firms know this and understand that the majority of junior associates will arrive at their offices without a clue as to what they want to do or what Biglaw firm work actually entails. For this reason, most firms allow junior associates to try out a few different practice areas as summer associates and during their first year on the job.

Take every opportunity your firm gives you to try out everything that even potentially interests you. It will be easy to weed out some areas of the law after only one assignment (just make sure it was the work itself that you didn't enjoy, and it wasn't just a bad experience with one lawyer – if that's the case, consider giving the work a second chance). I've never liked the idea of arguing in court before a judge, so I knew from the get-go that litigation was not for me. To narrow it down further, it took more time to understand what each specific practice group did.

As you take on new work and try to figure out whether you are interested in it or not, reach out to associates and partners and ask them questions about their practice areas. It will be easy to spot those who are genuinely interested in their field. These lawyers read articles about hot topics in the industry, on Saturday mornings (and they email you about them). You know those daily bulletins informing you of new updates in the industry or changes in the market? They read those, too. The Wall Street Journal and the Financial Times? Yep, they read those, too, and the list goes on and on. These lawyers not only read about their field; they actually want to talk about cases and regulations affecting their industry. They write articles and client alerts and share their knowledge, instead of waiting to see what others will say and following suit. These lawyers want to be industry leaders and they become so because they genuinely love their practice areas. That's the kind of lawyer you want to become, so your goal is to find the work that will spark that in you.

You will spend so many hours working in Biglaw that you owe it to yourself to put in the effort as a junior associate to find something that lights you up and will do so for the long-term. Don't settle for a practice area that is just "OK." If you hate litigation, make sure you find something you love as much as you hate litigation, not something that is just "not as bad." That will be a mistake in the long run and won't set you up for a sustainable career.

Do You Like the Day-To-Day Legal Work?

In addition to liking your practice area, you also have to like the day-to-day work and practical implementation of the law. For example, you may be fascinated with bankruptcy case law and love reading the Delaware Chancery Court's new rulings, but what about the work of an actual bankruptcy attorney? Do you like spending hours reviewing documents and parsing through responses? Do you like the idea of arguing in bankruptcy court, where the rules are not straightforward and which has been described as the "wild, wild west" of courtrooms, or would you prefer to practice in a more traditional courtroom setting like you would find in a typical litigation?

If you are intellectually interested in a field of law, but once you dabble in it and it turns out that you don't like the work, keep on looking until you find one you do like. Of course, you don't have to like *every* aspect of your day-to-day job (you very likely will not). Every practice area and job comes with those tasks that are annoying or that we don't like, but we put up with them and get through them so we can keep doing the work that we love to do.

How to Get What You Want

Once you've identified potential practice groups or lawyers you want to work with, you *must* be proactive to end up in a practice group of your choosing, doing the work that you want. If you let the system run its course, you will probably get a smattering of assignments from various groups, some of which you'll like and some of which you won't.

Don't just sit there and hope the work you want will come to you because it won't. If your firm has an assignment system where a coordinator assigns associates work, your firm might tell you not to seek out work outside of this system. Ignore that. This system is meant to be worked around, and everyone does it, so you should, too. Introduce yourself to the partners you want to work with and let them know you're incredibly interested in their practice area. Tell them why you want to work with them or why their field is so exciting to you. The next time something comes up that they need a junior associate for, guess who they are going to call or request? You, because they want to work with associates who want to work with them, too.

If you work with someone and you enjoy her work, tell her. Tell her you'd love to do more work with her group. Someone has to get the best assignments and someone has to get the work you want, so why not let that be you.

What Motivates You?

Finding work that you like and are interested in will motivate most of us to come to work every day and put in the effort to do a good job. But is that enough? Is work that you are interested in enough to keep you going late at night, on the weekends, and when you have to miss a significant life event to finish it? It might not be. Which is why there is something else you have to ask yourself as a Biglaw attorney: *Why* are you working in Biglaw?

This is probably a question everyone should ask herself or himself, but it's particularly important in Biglaw because of the sheer amount of time Biglaw attorneys spend at work. The question may be simple, but the answer and thought process needed to arrive at the answer are complex. If you don't have a "why" behind your reason to work it can be very challenging to stay motivated to do your best.

The question of "why" is a complicated one and many books have been written about finding your own particular "why" and life purpose. I recommend that you read some of these books and think about your overarching "why" – why are you a lawyer and why are you a Biglaw lawyer, in particular? Since that is a very personal question and one for you to tackle on your own, here we are going to talk about another aspect of your "why" – your daily motivation.

Most junior Biglaw associates are extremely hardworking individuals. They have worked hard their entire lives to get into the best colleges and law schools, make law review, and land a Biglaw job. Naturally, they are programmed to work hard. That work ethic will follow them into their careers at Biglaw. What motivates them? Most junior associates' daily motivation is to do a good enough job to survive their first year and make it to year two. By year two, hopefully, you will have found your place at the firm and will have a clearer idea as to what you want from your career.

When you reach this point and your head is finally above water, I suggest that you take a step back and ask yourself the following: when you work hard, spend all night finalizing a document, or spend your whole weekend drafting interrogatories, *why* did you do it? Why are you motivated to do your absolute best work, during the day-to-day moments that sometimes feel like a never-ending grind? Let's take the easy answer off the table right away: that it's your job and of course you do it because you get paid to, and if you didn't, you'd get fired. Instead, think about *why* you stayed in the office until 4:00 a.m., went home, slept for two hours, showered, and came right back to the office at 8:00 a.m. to put in another marathon day?

Early on in my career, it was easy for me to identify what motivated me to do great work. I worked hard because I respected the senior associates and partners I worked with so much that I wanted to do a fantastic job for them. I wanted to get the gold star, the A+ on the assignment, and I wanted praise from the people I was working with.

It didn't matter to me if a client did not acknowledge that I'd stayed up all night to revise a 250-page offering document which he had asked for just twelve hours before. What mattered to me was that my team at the firm, my fellow associates, and the partners I worked for, were happy with my work and with my efforts. Maybe I stayed that night so that the fifth-year associate on the team could go to her anniversary dinner. I knew that she would be grateful for this and that when a situation arose where I had something meaningful to go to, she would return the favor. Helping her was why I stayed and what motivated me.

As I became more senior, I started working less with the

partners and more directly with the clients. This is how your career is supposed to progress. The more senior you become, the less oversight you need and the more client interaction you'll have. As a senior associate, when I would send a document to a client, it would no longer have to go to the partner first to review. Instead, I would send it straight to the client. I was no longer working for my gold star from the partners but rather the gold star from the clients, and that is harder to get.

I was losing my daily motivation because the motivation I had to work for the clients was simply not the same as the motivation I had to work for my team. My daily "why" and daily motivation was fading away the more senior I became. What I realized was that I had little to no connection to most of my clients. Instead of feeling excited and challenged by the last minute requests they would send me, I felt frustrated and stressed.

Now, this is a very particular feeling that I had. Many people are motivated by other things. Some are motivated by getting the task done and knowing they did a great job, no matter if they receive praise or acknowledgment from anybody. Others are motivated by doing a fantastic job for the client and getting them out of a jam. Still, others find that their motivation is solving a complex issue. If your motivation is to work hard for your partners and fellow associates and only them, you will not survive in Biglaw long-term. You must develop a motivation to do good work that goes beyond getting approval or a gold star from your supervisors.

What is your motivation? Take some time to think about it. You don't have to know the answer today, but keep the question in the back of your mind and reflect on it often.

~ ~ ~

Use your time as a junior associate to try out as many practice areas as you can to make sure your interest in the field and in the day-to-day tasks of an attorney practicing in that niche align. You need these two things to be in sync for a successful, long-term career.

Not only do you have to find work that is interesting to you, but you also have to have a reason to get up and get to work to do that job every day. Figure out what motivates you to do a good job. As long as you stay motivated, you can succeed. If you feel that motivation slipping away, find new motivation or move on. You can't do your best work unless you are interested in it and motivated to perform at your best.

Chapter Fourteen

The Many Benefits of Pro Bono

Pro bono is some of the most valuable work a Biglaw associate can undertake. Helping an underserved or unrepresented population is why many of you went to law school in the first place. Somewhere along the way, possibly because of massive amounts of student loans and the lure of a six-figure salary to help make a dent in their repayment, many people who became lawyers to help marginalized populations end up in Biglaw instead. Even most who never intended to work full-time in the non-profit world are interested in using their legal skills for good, and pro bono is a way to accomplish this while still working in Biglaw.

When it comes to available resources, Biglaw is the ultimate place to practice non-profit law. From sending DHL packages around the world (I used to send documents to a remote village in Guatemala that, miraculously, always made it there and back) to having access to a partner who usually charges clients over $1,000 an hour to review a provision of your agreement, Biglaw spares no expense in representing its pro bono clients to the fullest.

While you won't be able to spend all of your hours doing pro bono work, there is an almost limitless amount of pro bono work available to you. So long as you get your billable work done, if you choose to devote extra hours to pro bono, you can. Pro bono cases are some of the most worthwhile experiences you will have in Biglaw and I encourage you to take on a few early on in your career to see what you enjoy. The pro bono cases I worked on during my eight years in Biglaw were the most rewarding work I did, not to mention some of the best learning opportunities.

Still, not all pro bono is created equal when it comes to how much value you can provide a client and how much value you can get out of it – both personally and professionally. Be strategic about what pro bono work you take on. In this chapter, you'll see why pro bono work is so valuable to your community and your career, and learn some tips on how to fit pro bono in with your billable hours.

Pro Bono Helps You Hone Your Legal Skills

Many of the things you'll do as a junior associate don't require a law degree, but you have to start somewhere. Hopefully, you'll work with people who give you substantive assignments, but even so, those will usually just be first drafts of something that will be reviewed by many more eyes before being sent to a client. Unlike your billable work, your pro bono work won't be scrutinized or reviewed by countless senior attorneys (with the exception of a partner or pro bono supervisor, who are usually just around for support on major issues, you'll be flying solo). Pro bono is your opportunity to take ownership of real, substantive work as a junior associate.

Junior associates have the opportunity to take on pro bono assignments on day one. Not only that, but you might be the only lawyer staffed on the entire matter. The beauty of pro bono, which can be intimidating at first, is that you won't have much oversight, if any, so you have total control over and full responsibility for your work. Pro bono is your chance to step up and hone skills that, in some cases, you would have to wait years to develop.

These are some examples of what you can do on a pro bono case as a junior associate that you would never do so early on in your career with billable work:

- Appearing in immigration court (which might consist of cross-examining witnesses, filing motions, and arguing in front of a judge) in an asylum case.
- Representing a mother in a contested custody case in family court.
- Drafting and negotiating corporate contracts for a start-up.
- Forming and incorporating a 501(c)(3) non-profit company.

You will also have some control over what type of pro bono work you do and, therefore, what skills you can focus on developing. As a corporate associate, if you hate the idea of appearing in court, you probably want to steer clear of a family law case that would require that. On the other hand, if you are a corporate associate, a family law case will probably be your only chance to see a courtroom, so you might want to seize that opportunity if it is something you'd love to experience. The same goes for a litigation associate. Pro bono may be the only time a litigation associate might draft a contract, so if that's something you're interested in doing, pro bono is your chance. Any pro bono assignment that you find interesting is bound to be beneficial to both your client *and* your career, no matter what area of the law it falls under.

Pro Bono Allows You to Expand Your Network Within the Firm

Another benefit to pro bono work is that you can expand your circle within your firm and work with people you normally never would. Biglaw firms are enormous places with hundreds of lawyers, but most lawyers work with the same people over and over again.

Pro bono is a great way (and likely one of the few ways) to work with your friends and colleagues in other groups at the firm. As a first-year associate, I worked with a friend from my summer associate class on an immigration case. He was in the IP litigation group and we never worked together on anything else again, but it was nice that I got to work with him that one time. Remember in the *Preface* where we talked about how you would have no idea what your colleagues in other groups of the firm did all day? Well, pro bono might be your only chance to learn from them.

Pro bono is also a great way to strategically work with those you'd like to work with on billable matters in the future. At my firm, a top M&A partner was very involved in the firm's post-conviction justice project. This would be the perfect pro bono project for an associate who had an interest in M&A and who wanted the opportunity to work directly with this partner who she might otherwise not have direct access to. By working on the pro bono project and showing her dedication and abilities, she could put herself on his radar, develop a good working relationship, and parlay that into billable work.

Pro Bono in the Eyes of Others

Biglaw firms are proud of the pro bono work they do, and rightly so. Your firm will probably encourage its associates to take on pro bono projects, with some even requiring a certain minimum of pro bono hours per year. However, this does not mean that every partner at the firm values the time you spend on pro bono work. Just because all of the firm's resources will be behind you on your pro bono projects doesn't mean all of the firm's partners will be. He might not say it directly, but it will become apparent when a partner you work with does not view your pro bono project as worthwhile but rather as something that takes you away from your billable work.

During my first year, I was very involved with an immigration project, which included attending clinics in the Bronx one evening a month to give free immigration consultations. I had to leave the office around 6:30 p.m. one evening to make it to the clinic on time and I told the partner I was working with when I had to leave, assuming that since we weren't doing anything urgent that it would be fine. He said it was fine, but as 6:30 p.m. approached and I sat in his office reviewing documents we didn't need to finalize for another week, I began to get anxious. Finally, at 6:45 p.m., I reminded him I had the clinic and he let me go.

I had incorrectly assumed that he viewed my pro bono work with just as much importance as our billable work. While I thought – and still think – that pro bono work is just as valuable as billable work, he didn't, and that's OK. Everyone is entitled to their own view of pro bono work and its value. This story isn't meant to deter you from pro bono work in the slightest or to slam those partners who don't think you should do it. Instead, it's a reminder that when it comes to pro bono work, the firm's official message doesn't necessarily trickle down to every associate or partner at the firm. You will work with partners who do not value your pro bono work. When you do, accept this and never let them feel like your pro bono work conflicts with their billable work or takes you away from doing what they consider your "real" job.

For every partner like the one I just described, there is at least one partner who is as passionate about providing excellent, free legal work to clients in need as he is about delivering top-notch billable work. A partner I worked with devoted countless hours every year to pro bono, going above and beyond the call of duty and treating his pro bono clients in the same way he treated his high-paying clients. We once had an all-day meeting with our pro bono client on the Friday before Memorial Day because that was the only time she could come to our office. Instead of complaining that he was working for free on a holiday weekend, when most other partners had long fled to their beach houses, he prepared for and devoted himself to this meeting like he would the most important client of the firm.

If you plan to devote a lot of time to pro bono work, it's best to work with people on your day-to-day billable work who also support and do pro bono. If a partner doesn't do pro bono work himself, it's less likely that he places much value in it. This is just another factor to consider when you are a junior associate deciding which practice group you want to be in or which partners you want to work for long-term. Do you want to be in the group that puts billable hours above everything, or do you want to be respected for your pro bono work as well? Look to the leaders in that particular group and see what they do. This can be extrapolated beyond pro bono work to include other non-billable firm commitments you might want to participate in. If the partners do pro bono, participate in summer associate events, serve on firm committees, and generally seem like good "firm citizens," they will probably be more accepting of your other endeavors inside the firm. Let this help guide you when looking where and with whom you want to work.

~ ~ ~

Pro bono work was some of my favorite work at the firm and I highly recommend finding a project that will fulfill you and teach you essential skills. Just remember that not everyone in Biglaw views pro bono in the same light. If you can find a team to work with on your billable work, which also respects pro bono work, all the better.

Chapter Fifteen

The All-Important Self-Evaluation and the Equally-Important Self-Assessment

As described in the *Preface* and touched upon elsewhere in this book, if you let it, Biglaw will take you along for the ride: its ride, not yours. It is easy to get swept up in the daily rush of client demands and firm responsibilities and forget that you ultimately have control over your career and where you want to take it. At the beginning of your career, it can be challenging to step back and see the big picture of where you are headed. There are two key ways you can support yourself as you navigate your Biglaw ride.

The first is through the self-evaluation, which most firms require associates to complete once a year and submit before their formal annual review. The second is what I call the self-assessment, an entirely voluntary process you use to look at your career progression and check in with where you stand by asking yourself: are you satisfied and fulfilled with your career and do you see a future for yourself at the firm? Let's first dive into the self-evaluation and we'll turn to the self-assessment next.

What Is the Self-Evaluation?

Before a formal annual review, most firms require every associate to fill out a self-evaluation. These typically consist of both written responses, detailing what you accomplished over the past year and outlining what you hope to achieve in the year ahead, as well as scaled responses, where you evaluate yourself in various categories on a scale of one to five.

The self-evaluation serves two purposes: one is for you, the associate, and the other is for the firm. For the associate, the self-evaluation is used to evaluate yourself against the firm's benchmarks set out for your class year and to set goals for the upcoming year. For the firm, the self-evaluation is used to compare the associate's perception of herself with the firm's opinion of her performance. Ultimately, the self-evaluation is used by both groups (the associate and the firm) to check in with each other and make sure the expectations, performance, and goals align.

How to Complete the Self-Evaluation So That You Benefit From It

The self-evaluation is, first and foremost, a tool for you to use. Unfortunately, most associates do not spend enough time completing their evaluations, and I fell into this camp myself for a couple of years. It can be tough to complete it in a thoughtful way when you are swamped with work, but try to find the time for it. It might be helpful to think of it as a tool for yourself as opposed to yet another firm requirement. Here are a few ways to complete the self-evaluation so you get the most out of it.

1. Use the Firm's Benchmarks to Highlight Your Skills, Find Gaps in Your Knowledge, and Set Goals

When it comes to evaluating yourself, the firm's published benchmarks are an excellent place to start to get a sense of just how well you are doing. Most firms put together guidelines, listing out various milestones you should be reaching, for both associates and the firm to gauge whether associates are developing the skills the firm is expecting of them at an appropriate time.

For example, a second-year litigation associate might be expected to have sat in on a deposition or prepared a witness for one. More generally, all second-year associates, both in litigation and in corporate groups, will be expected to have developed the instincts to know when an issue requires senior attorney supervision or help as opposed to being something the associate can solve on his own.

Highlight Your Skills

Refer to the benchmarks to gauge where you stand against where the firm thinks you should be. Review these to remind yourself of any specific skills or accomplishments that you are particularly proud of that you'd like to highlight during your review. The benchmarks can help jog your memory as to all you've learned, know how to do, and want to make the firm aware of.

Are you a third-year M&A associate who is expected to have led a large-scale due diligence project by this time? If you have done so, include details on this project in your self-evaluation to highlight to the firm that you are successfully hitting your benchmarks. Sometimes you only get one chance a year to meet with the partners who lead the group, conduct the reviews, and make decisions that impact your career. If there is something you want them to know, include it here.

Find Gaps in Your Knowledge

On the other hand, if you haven't accomplished a particular task or skill yet, consider why not. If you are a second-year associate in the litigation group and have not yet prepped a witness for a deposition but are expected to have done so, reflect on why you haven't. There are many legitimate reasons why you might not have reached all of the benchmarks, but it's nevertheless good to evaluate why not.

Was it because you were busy staffed on other projects that overwhelmed your workload this year, was it because you didn't seek out the proper work, or was it because you weren't yet trusted to prep a witness? If you are honest with yourself, the answers can be quite revealing. This might bring something up that you should ask about during your evaluation. For example, if you've been asking for work but aren't getting enough, bring this up during your evaluation and ask what's going on.

Set Goals for the Upcoming Year

The self-evaluation also usually includes a section where you set goals for yourself for the upcoming year. These can range from skills you want to acquire (like taking a deposition or leading a conference call) to people you want to work with to a new type of assignment you'd like to try. This is your chance to put on the record what you'd like to accomplish over the next year.

If nobody knows you're looking for a certain kind of work or are trying to develop a certain skill, nobody will give that work to you or make sure that development happens. Be proactive. There's no guarantee that you'll get what you want, but if you never ask, you'll certainly never get it. Look at the firm's benchmarks for the class year ahead of you to get ideas if you aren't sure what goals to set.

2. Don't Sell Yourself Short

Many of us tend to sell ourselves, our accomplishments, and our hard work, short. Your self-evaluation is not the place to be humble. No matter how hard it is for you to be positive about yourself and your skills, you do yourself a disservice if you don't play up all of the ways you contribute to the firm. Leave nothing out, and that includes all of your non-billable work, too. Whether it is the mentoring program you are a part of, the pro bono project you are devoted to, the firm committee you chair, or anything else, include it in your evaluation. Brag a little. These self-evaluations, along with the firm's written evaluation of you, will go into your permanent HR file, so include anything you want to make its way into your record.

This brings us to another standard piece of the self-evaluation: the scaled responses section. You'll be presented with a series of statements or questions and will have to rate yourself on a scale of, for example, one to five, with one being "needs significant improvement" to five being "excels at this skill" (you get the idea: one is terrible; five is fantastic).

During my first couple of years as a Biglaw associate, I agonized over these questions and how to grade myself. Did my communication skills warrant a four? Or maybe I was really a three since I sometimes got nervous when I had to talk to clients, right? I certainly was not a five, so back and forth in my head I would go, vacillating between a three and four in most categories, ultimately landing on a three and vowing to work on that skill the following year. I probably rated myself mostly fours, giving myself threes for things I felt particularly bad at, and fives only for categories like "firm citizenship," which I felt confident in given the amount of non-billable time I spent on recruiting, events, and things of that nature.

My approach to these scaled self-evaluations changed for the better when I was a fourth-year associate and a coworker in my group who had recently made partner said something that stuck with me. He was always super confident and I envied his natural ability to come across as knowledgeable and competent. One evening, a group of associates was chatting after a firm cocktail party about the self-evaluations that were due the next day. He was baffled when someone mentioned struggling with how to rate himself.

What was it that puzzled him so much? He said that when he used to fill them out as an associate, he always gave himself fives across the board. In his opinion, he worked tirelessly for the firm and was excellent at what he did, so why would he be anything less than a five? If he deserved a rating of anything less than a five in any category, the firm would surely tell him what they thought he needed to work on and he would. His point was: why would he give himself low marks if he knew he was a rock-star associate? He told us that nobody ever commented on his extremely confident self-evaluations. I don't have any evidence to back up his approach, other than the fact that he made partner and continues to thrive at the firm to this day.

In my self-evaluation the next year, I took his advice to heart and I agonized way less over my self-evaluations from there on out. I was doing my best work and if the firm thought I could do something better, they would surely tell me, so why put myself down in my own evaluation? Which brings me back to the beginning point of this section: don't sell yourself short in any part of the self-evaluation, whether it is in your written responses or the scaled responses. Stick up for yourself and use the self-evaluation to share with the firm just how great you are.

What Is a Self-Assessment?

The self-evaluation is something you *have* to do (that, if done right, can serve you well), whereas the self-assessment is something you will *want* to do (after reading this chapter). The self-assessment is an entirely voluntary assessment of your career. It's not firm-sponsored or firm-produced like the self-evaluation and won't go into your HR record or be shared with anyone (unless you want to share it). Here's why it's even more critical than the self-evaluation.

As a Biglaw lawyer, your job will take up the majority of your waking hours. That's just a fact. Because your job is such a significant part of your life, you must continuously evaluate your work to make sure you are working on what you want to do. Otherwise, you may find yourself devoted to a practice group or niche that you never wanted to be in and don't have any interest in. It also becomes very easy to forget about all other aspects of your life when Biglaw is crying out for your attention all of the time.

This is where the self-assessment comes in. Ideally, you will go through the process outlined in this chapter every quarter for the reasons described below. Even if you only do it annually or whenever you happen to remember to do it, completing a self-assessment will put you a step ahead in terms of planning your career and your life.

How to Complete a Biglaw Self-Assessment

This is how you complete a Biglaw self-assessment: every quarter, you take stock of your job and your life by asking yourself the following three questions and recording your answers:

1. Do You Enjoy Your Work?

If you do, then, great! You're probably right where you should be. If you don't enjoy the work you are doing, seek out new work. Maybe try out a new area of the law (if you're still junior, there's some flexibility in what you can do) or ask for a new type of assignment.

2. Do You Like the People You Work With?

If you do, then, great! If you don't like the people you work with, seek out work from a new group or a new partner, who likely works with different associates. Every small group in a firm has its own style. Don't stop looking until you find the one that is a good fit for you.

3. Do You See a Future for Yourself at the Firm?

If you do, then, great! While it is often hard to see a future at the firm when you are a junior associate and there are so many unknowns at play (both within your control and out of your control), such as whether the market will be strong enough to support another partner when your time comes, you have to at least see that *possibility*. If you don't see a future for yourself at the firm, start making plans for your future somewhere else.

Putting It All Together

Put your answers to these three questions together: if you enjoy the work, like the people you work with, and can envision yourself at the firm a few years into the future, you are in a good place. On the other hand, if the answer to any of these questions is that you dislike the work, don't get along with your colleagues, or would be disappointed if you were to wake up in a year or two and find yourself sitting at the same desk and doing the same thing, it's time to put the wheels in motion to plan a career change.

You will get the most out of this exercise if you do the self-assessment every quarter. If not, too much time might pass by before you realize that you've become miserable, or are on your way there. Another reason why it's important to do these quarterly assessments is because of the year-end bonus that law firms dangle in front of their associates who hit their required billable hours. If you are ready to leave your job, but won't admit this to yourself until July or later in the year, you will have likely already put in over 1,000 hours of billable time, or 50% of the required hours to get a bonus. Once associates hit 50% of their required hours and half of the year's work is done, they often reach a point of no return: it doesn't make much sense to quit at that time when so much has already been invested. And so another six months go by. Then when the bonus hits their bank account (usually in December or January), they get a little ego boost and suddenly the firm they disliked so much a few weeks ago doesn't seem so bad anymore. Don't let the bonus or compensation of any form stop you from making a career move you want to make.

~ ~ ~

The yearly self-evaluation may be the only time you can voice, on record, your opinion of your performance. Even during your busiest seasons of work, take the time to complete it, thoughtfully, for your own sake. Becoming aware of your strengths and areas you might need some work on will do nothing but help you clarify where you are and where you want to take your career. And don't sell yourself short, ever. You were smart enough to land a Biglaw job so you are smart enough to be there. Don't forget that. The self-assessment is your chance to be honest with yourself and gauge your situation. Are you satisfied with where you are or is it time to make some moves? Without a periodic (hopefully, quarterly) in-depth look, you risk letting time pass you by without making any plans.

By doing the self-evaluation in conjunction with the self-assessment, you'll gain clarity and create a big picture for yourself of what benchmarks in your career you are hitting, where you need to improve, and where you want to take yourself over the next few years.

Chapter Sixteen

How to Take a Vacation

What do you imagine when you picture yourself on vacation? Most of us see ourselves relaxing on the beach, skiing in the mountains, or just being with family and enjoying down-time. For a Biglaw junior associate, vacations can be just that – a glorious time away from the office – but they can also be confusing and stress-inducing.

The words "vacation" and "junior associate" will elicit very different responses from senior lawyers at a Biglaw firm. Whether junior lawyers "deserve" to take vacations is a hotly contested topic. Some senior attorneys in Biglaw think that junior associates, who have barely begun their careers, haven't put in enough time or sacrifice and haven't proven themselves yet. Therefore, some argue, they shouldn't take a vacation until they've earned it. Others will have no problem with junior associates taking time off and will even encourage it.

Because of these differing opinions, Biglaw is a confusing place when it comes to vacation time and junior associates. While there will be policies in place and messaging from the firm encouraging you to take a vacation (from the HR department, your practice group's leaders, or the people you work directly with), do they really mean it? There's no way to know for sure.

But even if there is no way to know for sure if everyone you work with believes that junior associates are entitled to take vacations, listen to this clear message instead: you absolutely, 100% should take vacations as a junior associate and throughout your Biglaw career. Not only do you deserve it, but you also need it, even as a junior associate who hasn't necessarily worked for that many years. It shouldn't take three years to earn a vacation. Biglaw demands a *lot* of your time. Vacations allow you to recharge and help you stay sane in Biglaw longer than if you never took time away.

How to Prepare for a Vacation

Unlike some workplaces where all you need to do to prepare for a vacation is put your planned time off into a calendar or clear it with a supervisor a few weeks in advance, there is an art to taking a vacation in Biglaw. Not only do you need to plan ahead, but you need to prepare in a very specific way so that you can return from the vacation having had a real break and feeling refreshed. Here are some strategies you can follow as a junior associate to make that refreshing return a reality.

1. Tell Your Team as Far in Advance as Possible

Nobody likes to be surprised with the news at the last minute that his colleague will be out of the office on vacation for two weeks or even just a few days. Be respectful of your coworkers and let them know as far in advance as possible what your vacation plans are. It might feel silly to you to let them know that you'll be taking time off in a few months, but it is never too early to tell your team when you plan to be out. Maybe they won't do anything about it that early on, but maybe they will. There are staffing considerations partners plan ahead for that you might not be aware of, so it's always best to give everyone on your team – from the partner to the other associates – as much lead time as possible.

In addition to telling your team in person (which is helpful, but who is going to remember someone else's vacation plans when there are so many things to remember for yourself?), put it into your Outlook calendar and your team's shared calendar, if you have one (if you don't have one, you can suggest the team create one, as it's beneficial for everyone to be able to see who will be out of the office and when). As your vacation draws near, remind everyone of your planned time away. Don't worry about being annoying; by being proactive and forcing your team to plan for your absence, in the end, you will save everyone the hassle of scrambling to cover for you while you're out.

2. Keep Your Team in the Loop on Everything You Are Working On

In *Chapter Five*, we talked about the importance of keeping your team in the loop on all of your projects. This is especially true during the time leading up to a vacation. At least a week in advance of your planned time away, be extra sure to copy at least one other member of your team on every email you send and receive. Whenever you have an in-person meeting, conversation, or phone call with a client, the other side's lawyers, or other members of your team, include another team member. If that's not possible, give the relevant parties a status update of what was discussed shortly thereafter.

Organize everything you are working on so it will be easy for another person to find whatever document or piece of information they need to fill in. If you are in the middle of negotiating something or drafting a specific document, leave detailed information on its status so that whoever needs to pick it up while you are away will know exactly where it stands and how they can move it forward. The idea is to keep your work moving and make it as seamless a transition as possible.

3. Ask If Coverage Would Be Helpful and, If So, Find Quality Coverage

We've talked about how junior associates are generally interchangeable and replaceable. While that's true when it comes to beginning a new project, one junior lawyer is not interchangeable for another one once he is deeply involved on a matter. Even if your skill set and that of another first-year associate are essentially the same, once you've started working on something, you are infinitely more valuable to the team than someone who has no clue what is going on.

This means that finding coverage (i.e., asking another junior associate to work on the deal in your place while you are out) is not always helpful to a senior associate or partner. Still, before you leave for a vacation, you should always offer to find a temporary replacement. Sometimes the senior lawyer will take you up on that offer, in which case it is your job to find a junior associate who is willing to pinch in if needed (with the promise to her that you'll return the favor in the future) and also one you trust will be a quality team member.

4. Tell Your Clients

While you don't have to tell your clients as far in advance as you do your coworkers, if you are working directly with a client (either corresponding by email or phone relatively frequently), you should tell them your plans. A good rule of thumb for who you need to give the heads-up to is this: if you think they would be surprised to receive an out-of-office message from you, they should be told of your plans in advance.

Reassure the client that he will be in good hands with whoever it is who will be covering for you while you are out. Better yet, loop that person in on some of the work by copying her on all emails and introducing her to the client a few days before you leave. This way, the client knows who to contact, gets accustomed to her, and is not surprised or upset about your absence. Again, your goal is to make the work continue as seamlessly as possible while you're out.

There will always be clients, like some of those partners mentioned above, who give you attitude when you tell them you'll be out of the office. There is nothing you can do about that, other than giving them advance warning, providing them with good coverage, and reassuring yourself that you must be doing a great job if they are that upset that they won't be able to contact you and rely on your advice for a few days.

5. Tell the Lawyers on the Other Side, Too

While it is not required, it is courteous to give the lawyers from other firms you've been working with the heads-up that you'll be out. Let them know who to contact in your absence and who else should be included in correspondence while you're out. Not to beat a dead horse, but your goal is to make the process as streamlined as possible. The less uncertainty you leave behind, the better for everyone's sake (including your own).

6. Take a Buffer Day at the Beginning of Your Trip

The first five tips were mostly focused on preparing your team for your vacation to minimize how your absence will negatively impact them, the client, and the work. This tip is all for you: build in a buffer day at the beginning of your trip. Here's how this works in practice. Let's say you booked a vacation to Portugal and your flight leaves on a Wednesday. Tell your team, from day one, that you will be out of the office beginning on Tuesday. You don't have to lie to your team, but you don't have to share your exact flight schedule with them, either.

By giving yourself this buffer day, you will have a day to take care of any personal things you need to do before you leave. I cannot tell you the number of times I had an early flight to catch for a trip and found myself in the office until 3:00 a.m. the night before, desperately trying to wrap things up and get things in order. If I had given myself a buffer day, I would have avoided a stressful and sleepless start to my vacation.

It might seem like a waste of a vacation day, but building in this time to get your laundry done and your suitcase packed, and to tie up any loose ends, will be more valuable than an extra day at your destination that you can't enjoy because you are so exhausted.

What to Do While on Vacation

In my early days in Biglaw, people used to dream of (and sometimes succeeded at) taking vacations where there was no WIFI or cellphone service. Nowadays, truly off-the-grid locations are getting harder and harder to find, and it's getting harder and harder to convince others that you are really in a place with no service. A junior in-house counsel at our client once told me he was going to Napa Valley for the week, so he wouldn't have any cell service or email access. Even a few years ago this was laughable (really, no service in California?) and you could never get away with something like that now.

If there aren't many places left in the world that are remote and cut off from the internet, is there any way you can truly disconnect while on vacation? That depends mostly on the expectations of the senior members of your team. If they take vacations, but are always available and online working during those vacations, they might expect the same from you. Ask other associates what their experience is working with those people so you can prepare for how much, if any, work you will do while away. What I can say is that if you prepare for your absence and follow the previous tips, you'll at least set yourself up for the best chance to have uninterrupted time away. If you don't, you'll most likely be contacted with questions and will have to work. The effort you put in up-front will allow you the best chance to disconnect.

Everyone's experiences are different, but, for the most part, when I took a vacation in Biglaw, my time away was respected and all I needed to do was check my email once or twice a day to make sure nothing was "blowing up" in my absence. Most of my work while on vacation involved forwarding emails that were addressed only to me to another member of my team who was back at the office, and checking in once in a while to make sure everything was under control. While an entirely disconnected vacation would have been ideal, this limited amount of connection wasn't so bad either.

Coming Back to the Office

Remember that buffer day we talked about building into the beginning of your trip? Well, at the end of the trip, a buffer day is just as, if not more, important. When you set foot in the office after being away for more than a few days, your boss, even if she is well-meaning, will welcome you back with a huge pile of work. In her eyes, you were just away and should be refreshed and ready to get to work. In reality, you probably traveled all night the day before, are jet-lagged, and your brain wants to do anything but think about work. Nobody will be sympathetic to your jet-lag or post-vacation blues when they've been at the office the whole time you've been away.

Therefore, give yourself an extra day at home to get out of vacation mode and back into work mode. If you don't want to take a vacation day to do this, it works just the same to come back on a Saturday and treat Sunday as your buffer day. Do your laundry, buy some groceries, get a good night's sleep, and mentally prepare yourself for the next day. The transition back to work will go so much better if you do. When you do get back to work, thank your team for covering for you but also remember that you will cover for them in the future when they take their equally well-deserved time off, so you don't "owe" them anything but that.

Long Weekends

Taking a three-day weekend warrants its own section because it is where a lot of junior associates can get tripped up. When most people are junior associates, they are in their mid- to late-20s and are at a time in their lives where it seems as though every person they know is getting married, which means there are lots of weddings to attend and long weekends to take.

Your team will be willing to cover for you for some of these weekends, but it isn't wise to be *that* junior associate who constantly takes a Friday or a Monday off. It might sound harsh, but you need to make some hard choices when it comes to attending all of these events if you want to be viewed as a committed and reliable associate. This might mean missing a wedding or two, or skipping a Friday night rehearsal dinner so you can work on Friday when the rest of your team, partner included, will be spending the night at the office.

You absolutely can take the occasional long weekend, and it doesn't have to be as complicated as when you plan to take a more extended vacation, but it still needs to be done the right way. This means two things: clearing it with your team ahead of time and taking these days off sparingly.

Just like a more extended vacation, clear your day off with your team way ahead of time. To you, it's just a day, but missing someone for a day can be more disruptive to a team than missing someone for a week or two. If you are out of the office on vacation for a longer period of time, the senior person on the team will probably replace you during that time or will ask you to get coverage while you are out. When it comes to just a day or two, it's unlikely you will be replaced, since it's usually not worth it to bring someone up to speed for just a day's worth of work.

Coverage, therefore, is virtually useless for a short period of time and the senior associate will end up doing your work herself. This is part of what it means to work on a team – everyone, no matter what rank, covers for a team member when needed – but if you make a pattern of it and constantly take inconvenient days off, senior attorneys will not be happy with you.

Sometimes you will have to make a sacrifice and miss something you really wanted to attend. Biglaw is about sacrifices and choices, so be strategic about what you can miss and what you can't. If your second cousin is getting married in California, but you haven't talked to her in ten years, maybe skip that event and take a long weekend off for your best friends' upcoming wedding instead.

Getting Over the Guilt of Taking a Vacation

A feeling you are likely to encounter when you take a vacation is guilt. No matter how well and respectfully you prepared your team for your absence, you may feel like you are abandoning your work and leaving your team behind. How strongly you feel vacation guilt will depend on your personality, your office culture, and the overall vibe of your team.

That feeling of guilt might linger in the back of your mind during your vacation, or every time you check your email. Even if you covered for somebody the month before when she was on her well-deserved vacation, you will probably feel guilty when you check your email and see that she has been sending emails out on your deal at 4:00 a.m. You cannot help but feel guilty that she is up so late on account of your vacation.

Unfortunately, Biglaw doesn't do much to help you get over this feeling. I knew a partner who only took one real two-week vacation (for his honeymoon) during his fifteen-year and counting Biglaw career, and he wore this as a badge of honor. He never told anyone directly that they couldn't take a vacation (in fact, he encouraged taking vacations and would cover for associates when they were out on vacation), but just knowing that he never took time off created a certain culture around the office. It was one in which everyone felt guilty about taking a vacation, even if it was necessary and ultimately beneficial to the firm for them to recharge and come back to the office refreshed and better able to handle the stresses and demands of the job.

There isn't one perfect solution to getting over this vacation guilt. You will probably feel it, whether it is because others in your office project that onto you or the culture of the office doesn't support time off. But maybe it's not such a bad thing that there isn't an elaborate, step-by-step plan you need to implement to get over the guilt of taking a vacation. Perhaps, it's not that complicated after all. Take your well-deserved time away and do your best to leave the guilt behind.

~ ~ ~

Taking a vacation from Biglaw, whether it is a three-day weekend to the shore or a two-week adventure to Thailand, can be tricky. So long as you take your vacations the right way, by planning ahead and preparing your team and clients as best you can for your absence, you'll be able to get away from it all and will make for an even better employee and a more pleasant coworker once you're back. Push through any barriers you might be facing or guilt you might feel and take your vacations.

Chapter Seventeen

Remote Work Done Right

As I edit this book in the spring of 2020, we are in the midst of an unprecedented global health crisis that has left most of us confined to our homes. The coronavirus pandemic, with the epicenter of its U.S. outbreak in New York City (which also happens to be the epicenter of Biglaw), has forced businesses to shut down, restaurants to close, and offices to send their workers home to work remotely. I hope, when life eventually returns to normal (or our "new normal") and lawyers venture back to those big glass office buildings in Midtown Manhattan and around the world, that many lessons will have been learned about working from home. Working remotely, nevertheless, will remain complicated. How will remote work have changed when we come out of this? We just don't know the answer to that yet.

The advice in this chapter is based on a pre-pandemic world. Hopefully, we will have learned many things from our time apart and working remotely will have become more efficient and more generally accepted, but I imagine that a generational divide will remain. I am certain that the Biglaw hierarchy will remain. When we do get back to work in our offices, new associates will need to learn how to successfully balance face-time with remote work, just as those who came before them had to do. The advice to junior associates in this chapter will apply once again, at least until the world changes for good.

Navigating how to work remotely is complicated, especially for junior associates. When it comes to using modern technology, Biglaw is not exactly at the very forefront of the movement like companies such as Google, Apple, or Amazon are, but the legal industry is making progress. At most firms, associates have the technology and the permission to work from home, at least occasionally. If you are offered this opportunity, take advantage of it, but remember that working remotely is a privilege that should not be abused if you want to be viewed as a dedicated and dependable junior associate.

Remote work is ever-evolving as technology advances and new generations who are ever more used to technology in their daily lives enter the workforce. When I started in Biglaw as a summer associate in 2008, the firm gave us Blackberries and laptops. Technically, we could work from anywhere, but working remotely was very burdensome, time-consuming, and not practical, so it was hardly done. Now, however, technology has come such a long way that almost everything that used to have to be done in the office can be done remotely and seamlessly. You can answer calls from your office phone number so clients can't even tell that you are out of the office and you can join meetings via Skype, Zoom, or other videoconference tools. But just because you *can* work remotely does not mean you always should. The concept of "face-time" – being physically present in the office and showing your face – remains a vital aspect of Biglaw life.

A Generational Divide

Different generations working together in Biglaw have extremely different ways of viewing working from home. There are still plenty of partners and even some senior associates who were never able to work remotely when they were associates. Instead, they worked their way up by hand-marking up documents, using fax machines, dealing with actual paper originals, and waiting for late-night FedEx document deliveries.

In contrast to these generations, junior associates have grown up with technology and know their way around it as if it were built into their brains. This mix of generations working on the same matters can create tension between those who grew up without much technology and those who have always felt natural using it. There is also a push and pull between those who think junior associates have it too "easy" now and rely on technology too much, and those who believe we don't take advantage of all technology has to offer. If technology means people can work remotely, then why not let them?

This push and pull usually plays out like this. On one extreme, there are partners who think junior associates should be in the office at all times. These are few and far between, as even the more senior partners have begun to recognize that we can do many things remotely. On the other extreme, there are junior associates who think that because technology allows for it, they can work from home whenever they want. The truth falls somewhere in between. Even if you *can* use your phone and email the same way you could when sitting in the office, you are not as valuable, and sometimes not valuable at all, when you are not physically present in the office. Face-time is beneficial, but it doesn't need to be enforced strictly. There needs to be a balance.

The Value of Face-Time

Being physically present in the office with your coworkers provides benefits you just can't get when you are not together. Hopefully, these next few examples will shed some light on why many senior attorneys insist on your presence in the office and will help you understand that there is indeed some value to face-time.

1. Reading Your Coworkers' Faces

There is nothing like looking at a coworker during a meeting or a call and knowing precisely what he is thinking because you have spent so much time working together that you've gotten to know him so well. By spending time together, you learn how your coworkers react to different situations, can gauge their stress levels, and can decipher their level of understanding. It can be hard to tell just how much a junior associate understands what you've asked of him over the phone. In person, it is much easier to see if someone understands or if they are completely lost and need something to be explained in another way. None of this can be accomplished when you are not in the same room. Video conferencing helps, but it's not quite the same as an in-person meeting.

2. The Benefit of the Mute Button

You wouldn't believe how much strategizing goes on behind the scenes of a conference call. Meaningful conversations happen in the room when the mute button is hit. If you are not in the room, you miss out on all of this. So much learning in Biglaw goes on during a conference call, when you are in a partner's office and she puts the phone on mute to discuss what is going on. She might mute the call to ask you to check something, to explain what's going on, or to get feedback from you. All of these things can't be done if you aren't sitting right there with her.

3. Bonding With Your Coworkers

Being physically present in the office with your coworkers also allows you to bond with them. Coworking relationships can turn into genuine friendships in Biglaw, and those bonds are usually solidified by spending long days in a conference room, eating dinner at your desks together, or staying late to close a deal. Something is lost if you never experience some of these Biglaw rites of passage together.

The Value of Working Remotely – And How to Do It Right

Now that we've gone over some of the advantages of face-time and *not* working remotely, I'd be remiss not to mention some of the obvious reasons why working remotely can be so beneficial. From being able to see your kids for dinner to attending a doctor's appointment during the day to working in your PJs when you are too sick to come into work (or just don't want to cough and sneeze all over your coworkers), working remotely is a valuable tool and should be taken advantage of. Here are a few tips on how to successfully work from home.

1. Make It Easy for Your Coworkers

Some senior lawyers might have the preconceived notion that anyone who is working from home is less available and less productive than those working in the office. You can counteract ımption by doing everything in your power to make your ʒ remotely as seamless for your coworkers as possible.

This means investing in (if your firm does not provide it) and learning how to competently use all relevant technology. You should have a printer, office phone, monitor, and high-speed internet connection, and you should know how to connect them all. Basically, whatever you use in the office, you should have at home so that you can complete your tasks in the same efficient manner.

When working from home, take the time to prepare for the day and get yourself ready. Set up your workspace before business hours traditionally begin, do a test call from your work phone to your cell phone and vice versa, get your videoconference software set up, open up your relevant documents, and generally make sure everything you need for the day is available and is working properly. Doing all of this will make it easy for you to work seamlessly, thus not burdening your coworkers with your absence from the office.

2. Communicate in Advance

Where possible, tell your coworkers ahead of time what day or days you plan to work from home. Before your planned work from home day, remind them of it. If you can, arrange to work from home on predetermined days so your team gets into a routine (e.g., every other Thursday, or the first Monday of the month).

Of course, if you have an emergency come up that keeps you at home for the day, you cannot plan on working from home ahead of time. In this case, it is perfectly fine to let your team know in real-time that you will be at home and when during the day you will be unavailable to work (if you anticipate not being available the entire time).

3. Create a Real Workspace for Yourself at Home

Get rid of your distractions, which are different for every one of us. You know what they are for you. Is it a Bravo *Real Housewives* marathon? Don't just turn off the TV, unplug it. You can't be on a conference call and give 100% of your attention when you have Bravo on mute in the background (trust me, I've tried it before).

Do you find yourself constantly sneaking into the kitchen to cook breakfast, brunch, lunch, afternoon snack, pre-dinner snack, and so on? Close the kitchen door and only allow yourself to eat when you normally would eat at work. When working from home, it's impossible to eliminate all distractions but do your very best to limit them. If you have the space, get a desk or designate an area of the dining room table as your work station. Delineate your workspace from the rest of your home in any way you can.

4. Block out Your Calendar for Appointments

A common reason for working from home is so that you have time to run an errand, go to an appointment, or be around for a delivery or a handyman's visit. Everyone in Biglaw understands that this is why people take these days, and it is fine to have (short) periods of your day where you are not available. However, if you plan to be away from your computer, email, and phone for a few hours because, for example, you need to leave for a doctor's appointment, make sure your coworkers know this. No, they do not have to know where you are going, but they need to know when you aren't going to be responsive.

The easiest way to do this is to block off the time in your Outlook calendar. Give yourself a little buffer of time since appointments always tend to take longer than expected. If you are back early, great. Like most things in Biglaw, when it comes to your availability when working from home, it's always better to under-promise and over-deliver than the reverse.

Finding a Middle Ground

Now that you've read about the value of face-time and the value of remote work, it's up to you to find a middle ground and figure out what works for you, your team, and your firm.

Most firms have an office-wide policy for working remotely. Let's say your firm's policy is that you can work from home two days a month. Take advantage of that, but do not abuse it. Similarly, if you are sick, do not feel the need to come into the office and contaminate everyone. This a time where you absolutely should work from home, even if it's technically more days than your firm's policy allows.

It helps to look to those more senior in your office and on your team to see how they work. However, just because a sixth-year associate works from home, doesn't mean a second-year associate can do so in the same way. She might have a special arrangement with the firm or she simply might have earned the right because of years of hard work. You have to earn certain privileges in Biglaw, and that takes time.

The main issue for junior associates when it comes to working remotely is when they think that the flexibility that technology offers means that they have free rein to come and go as they please and to work from home whenever it suits them. Abusing this privilege will not be seen favorably by those more senior to you. Just because you *can* take an 8:00 a.m. call from your bed in your pajamas, does not mean that it is professional to do so or will further your career in any way if you choose to do so. When in doubt, get yourself to the office.

~ ~ ~

When and how to work remotely is one of the many choices you will make as you navigate life in Biglaw. If your firm allows you to work from home, by all means, take advantage of that. But, like many other choices in Biglaw, when in doubt, err on the cautious and conscientious end of the spectrum until you get a feel for how others on your team work. Part of your job as a junior associate is to be available, always, which also means being physically present in the office when a partner expects you to be. Not only will being in the office look good to those more senior to you, but you will also get to know your coworkers better and learn from them in ways you wouldn't be able to if you weren't physically there with them.

Chapter Eighteen

Be Professional, but Keep Your Personality

Working in Biglaw requires a high level of professionalism. I'm sure you've heard the standard rules before about professionalism: what to wear, how to interact with your superiors, how to address a client, and so on. I remember eating up all of that information when I was a law student, summer associate, and junior associate, and you should, too, especially if you've never worked in a professional office environment before. But what does it *really* mean to be professional?

What Does It Mean to "Be Professional"?

Being or acting like a professional means showing up on time, every day and to every meeting, being respectful of and courteous to your coworkers and clients, never missing a deadline, and producing consistently excellent work. Being professional does *not* mean that you have to create a wall between your office life and personal life and pretend that you don't have any interests outside of Biglaw. Because many Biglaw associates interpret "being professional" to mean this, they stifle themselves at work. In doing so, they essentially create a second personality for when they are at work and never show their true selves at the office.

In law school, I heard one tidbit of career advice that I grasped onto and took with me into my Biglaw career. I was told, "Whatever you do, do not bake cupcakes for the office." The advice came from a "career expert" who warned (women, mostly) against baking cupcakes for the office. Baking cupcakes represented office "housework," which includes things like scheduling meetings, cleaning up or organizing the supply closet, and remembering and baking for everyone's birthdays.

If you are seen as the office housewife, the argument goes, it makes it difficult to also be seen as a leader or as an equal to the men in the office. When I landed my law firm job, I decided that I would never bake cupcakes or cookies for my office. The problem was, I love to bake! During my first few years in Biglaw, not only did I not bake, for fear of being seen as the "office housewife," but I took this a step further and I held back in other ways. I thought the corporate world required me to hide my true personality, so I tried my very best not to be "too much." I toned down anything about me that was unrelated to work out of fear that showing that side would be unprofessional.

Eventually, after being in Biglaw for a few years, I let my guard down and let my personality creep back in. I opened up a little more to my coworkers and realized that you bond better and develop better relationships when you don't put up impenetrable walls. And guess what? I started doing better in my job and my career than I ever had. Those things that made me "me" also made me happier and more content at work. You might not realize it while you are doing it, but it takes a ton of effort to keep up a wall and hide your personality. When a wall goes up, you block not only what you deem to be the "bad" things, but the good things, too. Only when you allow yourself to break the wall down a bit can you begin to realize your true potential.

Don't let Biglaw's professionalism requirement suck your personality from you. There's room to be professional and keep your personality. Here are a few situations where it is OK to drop the super formal tone, kick outdated, bad career advice to the curb, and let your personality shine through, all while remaining professional.

1. Your Emails Don't Have to Be Formal All of the Time

When you email someone for the first time, whether it's a client, opposing counsel, or someone within your firm, it's best to err on the formal side. After a while, however, you can ditch the formal tone in your emails and just be *normal.* What does it mean to "be normal?" When I was a first-year associate, I was staffed on a deal with an associate just one year my senior. Despite having only one more year of experience than me, she insisted on reviewing all of my emails before I sent them out. She would make changes to all of my drafts, including making me do things like start my emails with "Dear X" and sign them, "Best regards," no matter who I was sending them to.

An email sent at 2:00 a.m. to a twenty-three-year-old investment banker who tended to respond with one-word answers, at best? Had to be formal. The partner we worked with and interacted with multiple times a day, in person, on the phone, and by email? Emails to him were formal, too. Luckily when that deal closed and I got the chance to work with more people, I realized that she was an outlier. Nobody else ever forced me into such unnecessary formality and almost nobody else I came across followed her extreme approach.

It is perfectly acceptable to address coworkers and clients informally after you've developed a relationship with them. That doesn't make you unprofessional, and neither does using exclamation points or smiley faces (yes, even if you are a woman). Don't be cutesy and informal if you are writing to someone you don't know or writing a serious email, but part of developing a rapport with your coworkers and clients is by acting *normal*! This also helps your clients get to know you, trust you, and like you. They won't connect with or trust a robot, so let a little bit of the "you" that makes you relatable, genuine, and trustworthy shine through in your correspondence.

2. Bring Personality Into Your Workspace

Most Biglaw firms generously offer even the most junior associates their own office space. You might share your space with another junior associate as a first-year associate, but within a few years of starting work, you'll most likely have your own office.

And because you'll have your own office space, you can do with it what you please, to an extent. Decorating your space is another opportunity to let a little bit of your personality shine through. Do you love bright colors, monochrome, or a minimalist look? No matter your design taste, make your space feel distinctly "you." For me, this meant having lots of colorful things in my office, from a gold desk lamp to bright watercolor paintings on the walls, to lots of flowers and plants. Not only did these decorations make me happy to be there, but having them also made me better able to focus, too, because I was surrounded by things that made me comfortable and put me at ease. If I was on an anxiety-inducing call, at least I was on the call from a comforting place.

For you, making your office your own could mean hanging photos of your family and friends, or putting up pictures of scenery from beautiful places you've vacationed or dream of going to. Maybe it means hanging your kids' artwork, a mural from a favorite museum, or something you painted yourself.

One caveat when it comes to artwork: when I was a first-year associate, we shared offices with one other associate. One of my coworkers was an amateur artist and she brought in one of her paintings to hang on the wall. The only problem was, it was a painting of a naked woman, and her officemate was not thrilled about this. After a mini-confrontation and discussion about what is "art," she agreed to take the painting home.

Everything you bring to your office is an opportunity to show people who you are. If it will cheer you up, brighten your day, remind you why you do what you do, bring you comfort, or otherwise make your life easier when sorting through piles of work, by all means, bring it in (just be respectful of your coworkers when making your choices).

3. Share Parts of Your Life With Your Coworkers

To an extent, keeping a separation between your work life and your personal life can be a good thing. There are some things that you probably want to keep private and out of the office. Your boss can know that you spent the weekend at your brother's bachelor party in Atlantic City, but he doesn't need to know the details.

Just let him know you had a great time, had some beers, saw a fun "show" and leave it at that. Being professional means having the discretion to keep some details of your life private. It does not, however, mean walling off your private life entirely from your work life.

Sharing pieces of your life lets you bond with your coworkers and gives you something to talk about. Sharing your plans also lets your colleagues know when something significant is going on in your personal life. While work will always come first in Biglaw, there are times when it is OK to be out of the office and times when your colleagues will cover for you. They can only cover for you, however, if they know that you are busy doing something important to you.

Make an effort to bring up details about yourself outside of work. Do you leave in the afternoon to pick up your kids at school? Is it your nephew's birthday on Saturday? Maybe your favorite sports team is playing that evening. Mention these things to your coworkers and ask them about their lives, too. One day, when something at work comes up that would have kept you in the office during an important time for you, your coworkers will be happy to cover for you if they feel connected to you.

Of course, there will be times where you will have to miss something, but by never mentioning your plans, you almost guarantee you'll miss them. It's not just about getting to go to an event or an appointment. If everyone knows you are a huge NY Jets fan, that, of course, doesn't mean you get a free pass whenever the Jets are playing. But maybe it means that a coworker will cover for you for a few hours when they know a key playoff game is on. At the very least, you'll show another layer of your personality to those you work with every day and will have something to talk to your coworkers about.

~ ~ ~

Whether it is in email, over the phone, or in person, a junior associate in Biglaw is expected to always be the consummate professional. But that doesn't mean you have to be stuffy and weird and turn yourself into someone else, or someone you think you should be. The world isn't going to end if you use an exclamation point or, god forbid, a smiley face in an email.

It's not unprofessional to let people in or show your true self and it's not unprofessional to have interests outside of Biglaw. Bake the cupcakes. Or whatever "baking the cupcakes" means for you. Whatever makes you "you," don't cover it up or hide it away at the office just because you think it will be bad for your career. More likely than not, letting your personality shine through will only help you succeed.

Chapter Nineteen

Taking Control at Work (Where You Can)

The lower you sit on the Biglaw food chain, the less control over your time you will have. As a junior associate, this means that Biglaw will take up a large chunk of your life, in a somewhat unpredictable manner. However, that does not mean that you have to hand over the keys to your career or your life. It means that you have to make some hard decisions and make a real effort to take control where you can. Some associates are naturally better than others at skillfully setting boundaries and carving out their own paths. This chapter and the following one (which focuses on making time for your non-Biglaw life) are meant for the rest of us: the people-pleasers who struggle with asking for what we want and setting healthy boundaries.

It's up to you to take control of your work by choosing what you do, what you work on, and with whom. With some planning, you can do this while still saying "yes" to almost everything the firm asks of you and building up your reputation as a reliable, excellent, and go-to associate. Here's what you can do to make this happen.

Getting the Right Amount of Work

Your firm will set its billable hours requirement, but you should also set your own. What is your personal goal? Do you want to hit 2,000 hours and not one hour more, ensuring that you remain in good standing with your firm and receive your year-end bonus? Do you want to be the highest biller in your group? Do you not really care and want to do as little as possible (not that this is an advisable or honorable goal, but it is the reality for some)? Whatever it is, figure out your goal and strategize about how you will reach it.

When it comes to billable hours, it's easy to set a goal, but not as easy to hit that goal. Things outside of your control, such as how much work you are assigned, influence this a lot. Fortunately, there are some things that you can do to increase the chances of reaching your personal target hours goal by the end of the year.

Is It Ever OK to Say "No" to Work? What If You Have Too Much Work?

There are a lot of messages out there right now about saying "no" to things that don't "spark joy" or don't interest you. This might be a good skill to have in life so you aren't taken advantage of or commit to things that you don't enjoy, but there isn't as much room in Biglaw to say "no," especially early on in one's career.

When *is* it OK to say "no" to work? If you are billing 80-100 hours per week, you can (and probably should) say "no" if someone tries to staff you on a new matter that will take up an additional forty hours of your time per week. Not many partners (although I won't go as far as to say none) would look down on you for saying that you cannot take on more work, so, by all means, say "no." But you cannot say "no" to assignments or requests just because they don't interest you or aren't convenient because they require weekend work. Reserve your "nos" for when the number of hours you are working backs up the claim that you are at capacity and cannot take on a new matter. If not, suck it up and do the work.

Make sure that if you say "no" to work right now, you aren't giving up opportunities to do that work in the future. If it is for a partner or group that you have been dying to work with, then buckle up and say "yes," even when you think you can't. Work your tail off so that you can do both your current work and your new assignment. If not, while some lawyers might come back to you in the future for a second assignment, most probably won't, and you'll never get the shot at working with them. They will have moved on to working with another associate and you might have lost your only opportunity, so think carefully before declining work that you've been waiting for.

Additionally, before you say "no" to work, make sure that you'll be busy enough later on in the year to hit your hours. Sometimes you have to take on more work than you want right now because the ebb and flow of Biglaw means there will come a time where you won't have any work at all. Prepare for these times. You usually have to be "on pace" to over-bill for the year just to reach your hours because there will be stretches of time when you don't have anything to do. Hardly anyone in Biglaw consistently bills forty hours every week.

What If You Don't Have Enough Work?

On the flip side, what if you don't have enough (or any) billable work? We talked about that in *Chapter Ten*, but here are some more tips. Continue to show up at the office, and show up on time. If your firm's business hours are 9:30 a.m. to 5:30 p.m., show up to work at 9:30 a.m. and stay for the entire day. You can take breaks, run errands, or go to the gym if you truly have nothing to do, but you should generally be present at the office during business hours. While some firms and groups have very lax standards as to when an associate should be in the office (especially if they worked late the night before), if you are not working on anything, that means you should arrive on time.

If you've just come off of a massive litigation or closed a deal and have been working hard for weeks or months, it's OK to take it easy for a bit. If that's not the case, or your last project ended a while ago and you've been idle for some time, you must be proactive. Don't just sit in your office by yourself for eight hours a day (people might think you're busy). Make it known that you need work and ask around, whether that is to an assignment coordinator, partners, or associates in your group. Aside from extreme circumstances such as a global recession or pandemic, it's your responsibility to keep yourself busy with an appropriate number of billable hours.

Why It's So Important to Choose Who You Work With

When joining a practice group or team, there are two main factors to consider. Do you like the work (which we talked about in

Chapter Thirteen) and, just as important, do you like the people you work with? Someone in charge of the junior associates will likely coordinate what work is available to junior associates, which associates are available, and who gets what work. In the first few months of work, you will get what you get, but beyond your first few assignments, you will have a say in not only what you are working on but who you are working with.

After you've found a couple of types of work you consider appealing, find the right people to work with. Your choice can make all the difference between a satisfying and a miserable Biglaw career.

Are You Working With People Whose Lives Look Like One You Would Want for Yourself One Day?

Some people can overlook working with difficult people. For others, the people themselves and their work styles and personalities make all the difference, and their job satisfaction has less to do with the actual legal work itself. Others take what is arguably the best approach for long-term success and look for a mix of the two: good work and good people.

We've already talked about finding work that is interesting to you. Put that together with finding people you work well with and who have the types of lives outside of work that you would like to have for yourself in the future. If you work with people who never seem to leave the office, never make it to their kids' events, and haven't seen a gym in years, they will probably expect the same from you. While it's possible to carve out time for yourself when working with this kind of person, it can be difficult if they expect you to behave in the same way they do (i.e., total devotion to the firm). Senior lawyers who do have outside interests, talk to you about them, and make the time for them, are more likely to accept your desire for some time away from work and will help you fit in that time away.

There is one caveat to note here: don't assume that because a partner or senior associate has what appears to be a somewhat balanced life, that means you can have that exact life, right now. As a junior associate, you have to earn your right to a more flexible and balanced schedule, which means putting in the time at work and at the office. You work the hardest now and sacrifice the most now so that you get the chance for more balance and control in the future.

Are You Working for the Right People?

What is your Biglaw goal? Don't worry if you don't have a clear picture yet, but keep your end goal in the back of your mind as you are deciding who to work with. Certain partners hold more powerful positions in the firm than others, and the associates who work with them, therefore, have more standing at the firm. If you're looking for long-term success and maybe partnership, you'll want to seek out certain partners. Contrast them with a fifteenth-year senior associate (yes, these exist) who will never make partner. He is probably less respected and works on less notable deals, so perhaps he isn't the best person to align yourself with. Of course, this all depends on what your end goal is at the firm, but keeping your options open for a long-term career is never a bad idea.

Remember, too, that if you are looking for a sponsor like we discussed in *Chapter Four*, it's all the more important to find the right person to align yourself with and work for as early on in your career as possible. That way, you can develop a sponsor-protege relationship naturally.

What to Do If You Get Stuck Working With Someone Awful

Sometimes you will get staffed on an assignment with someone, or maybe even a whole team, with whom you simply do not click. Don't expect to fit in with everyone. Some people won't like working with you and vice versa, and that does not mean your career has to end. It just means you have to find others to work with that you mesh well with, and sometimes that takes a few tries.

If you get staffed on something terrible with someone awful: power through the assignment as best you can, and seek out work from other senior attorneys and other groups while that matter is finishing up. Make yourself too occupied, and stay that way, to work with that difficult person or team again.

You can also do a couple of things to prevent getting stuck with that team or person repeatedly. Tell another partner that you prefer his work. Depending on your relationship with him and his relationship with the partner you disliked working with (be careful with this), you can be more or less open with how the other deal went. Never talk trash about a partner to another partner, but you can diplomatically mention that it is not your preferred type of work and that you would like to be staffed on something else going forward.

Be comforted by the fact that, so long as you aren't constantly unable to work with others (i.e., it has become a pattern that you have a problem with every person you get staffed on a matter with), it is OK not to click with everyone you work with. The good thing about Biglaw is that it is big; you will find your niche, eventually.

How to Take Control of Your Time While at the Office

There's lots of talk about how to protect your personal time, both in the Biglaw world and in the corporate world in general. Less talked about is how important it is to protect your time while at the office. If you don't protect your time at work, you'll never leave the office, and you won't even have any time away from the office to protect.

You have to get your work done while you are at work. Of course, some work will spill over into late nights and the weekend; that's the nature of Biglaw. But if you are not efficient during the workday or whenever you are at the office, are constantly distracted by your coworkers, or are pulled into one unnecessary meeting after another, you will have a very difficult time carving out any time away from work.

When you are in the office, be strategic about how you get your work done. Everyone develops their own methods and work styles over time, but even in the beginning, there are little things that you can do to save yourself hours of time. Below are some things that you can do to make your life easier. Depending on what type of law you practice, you may or may not be able to adapt these to your work life. You don't have to implement all of these tactics, but, hopefully, these examples will give you inspiration for solving any time management problems you encounter.

1. Prepare for Your Next Day the Night Before

Some advice books (even Biglaw ones) will tell you to set a cut-off time for work, say, 7:00 p.m., and prepare for your next day at that time. This is not practical advice because rarely will you be able to decide ahead of time when your day will be over (unless you have an arrangement with the firm to leave at a particular hour every night for childcare, for example, where you then sign back online later in the evening). You can, however, still prepare for your next day, no matter what time you leave the office.

When I was swamped with work, especially when I was at the office late at night, I found that even though I was exhausted, it was always a good idea to prepare for the next day before I left, no matter what time it was. I often took the last half hour or so to prepare myself for the day to come and was always thankful when I came into an organized workplace, especially after having slept very little the night before.

My preparation process involved some combination of cleaning up my office, throwing out useless documents, printing out the documents I planned to review, and sending charts to word processing to be formatted overnight. Whatever it is that helps set you up for work the next day, do it. Your future self will thank you when you arrive at the office the next morning with a fresh workspace and clear inbox.

2. Manage Your Email Distribution Timing

You don't have to send every email the second you finish drafting it. Prepare a few non-urgent emails at night before you leave the office, but don't send them yet. Save them in your email draft folder to send the next morning or set an automatic timer to send them at a pre-determined time. While it has become the norm to send and receive emails at all hours, you're not doing this to spare the recipients a late-night email, but rather to save yourself. If you send an email out at 2:00 a.m., the recipient might arrive at the office early the next morning, so by the time you arrive at the office at 9:30 a.m., after not much sleep, your client will have already responded and new emails and tasks will have already piled up.

To give yourself a break, hold off on sending non-urgent matters until the next morning or when you'll have more time to deal with the responses. That way, you can space your work out and won't fall behind on yet another matter before you even walk in the door. It's a simple way to control your workflow that really works and opens up more space for yourself than you would think.

3. Use Your Calendar Wisely

Your Outlook calendar, which others within your firm will probably have access to (they won't be able to see the appointment details, but they'll be able to see when you are busy in meetings and on calls), is your secret weapon. In addition to scheduling your meetings and calls, you should also schedule time for yourself throughout the day and block that time off as "busy" or "in a meeting" in your calendar.

"Time for yourself" doesn't mean time for personal tasks (more on that in the next chapter). It means quiet time to get your work done. Some days you will be so busy and your calendar will be so filled with other people's meetings and agendas that you won't be able to get any of your own work done. All of a sudden, it will be 8:00 p.m. or later and you won't have had a moment to turn to your overflowing email inbox or the draft document you need to submit by the end of the night. Even on the busiest of days, if you schedule in thirty minutes here or there for yourself, to check in on your to-do list, review your emails, and maybe even to start an outline of a draft, you'll have more control over the outcome of your day and will be able to get more work done.

4. Take Breaks but Don't Waste the Day Away

Taking periodic breaks throughout the day is essential if you don't want to burn out. We aren't machines and hardly anybody can sit at their desk for twelve, fourteen, or more hours a day and be productive that entire time. Build in breaks to grab lunch or coffee or to go for a quick walk around the block, but don't take too many. If you spend your whole day chatting with your fellow associates about how busy you all are, nobody can get anything done.

Don't linger for too long in your coworker's office after a call is over just to chat. Lunch breaks are necessary, but a three-hour summer lunch means three hours you'll have to spend at the office that night. A half-hour here and another hour there, and all of a sudden you will find yourself adding hours to your day that you have to make up for in billable hours later that evening. Strike a balance between much-needed breaks and work.

5. Find a Quiet Place to Work That Isn't Your Office

If your office building has space, find somewhere other than your own office where you can be productive. Isolate yourself in a cubicle in the library, in an unused conference room on another floor, or on a couch in a hidden lounge. Whatever it is, find somewhere that you can essentially "hide" and get some work done. Without the distraction of your phone or people popping by your office to chat or ask a question, you will be able to focus and get so much done in a short amount of time. Of course, you can't isolate yourself for a whole day, but taking a half-hour or whatever you can spare during which your clients and coworkers won't miss you, can lead to a big payoff in your productivity. The more you get done at work during business hours, the less you have to get done at home, on the weekend, or late at night.

~ ~ ~

How much work is enough? How much is too much? Too little? What should you work on and who should you work with? How are you supposed to get your work done when there's always something else to do or someone else to call? There's no simple answer to any of these questions, but, hopefully, this chapter has helped you realize that you do have a lot of choice and say in the matter when it comes to all of these situations. If you take the time to craft a career and work-style that suits your goals, you'll be more likely to enjoy your time in Biglaw.

Chapter Twenty

Your Unbillable Life: How to Manage Your Time Outside of Work

In Biglaw, the billable hour rules all. So much so that an entire chapter of this book is devoted to it. As a junior associate, your primary focus will be to log as many billable hours as you can, aiming for about 2,000 hours a year. As we have discussed, a certain number of those hours (up to about 200) can be taken up by non-billable work and still count toward your 2,000-hours requirement. These non-billable hours include time devoted to things like pro bono work and firm committees.

Lawyers are used to documenting their productivity and lives in six-minute increments, but, how about all of the other hours in a year? Under what category do those moments fall? All additional time spent physically at the office that is neither billable nor non-billable essentially doesn't count (from the firm's perspective). Not to mention your time spent *not* at the office, which is neither billable nor non-billable (unless you are working from home). It is as if that time doesn't exist because, although the time certainly passes, if you can't record it in your time entry as either billable or non-billable, it doesn't count in the eyes of the firm. If you aren't careful, you will start to discount that time, too.

I call this time "unbillable time" and the life you create outside of your billable life is your "unbillable life." Even inside the office, unbillable time is absolutely necessary for success. It's the time spent getting coffee with friends, eating lunch at the office cafeteria, and spending hours upon hours hanging out at happy hours and events with people you can hopefully call lifelong friends. Outside of the office, unbillable time is everything non-Biglaw related in your life that takes place after work and on the weekends. It's the time you spend with your family and friends, on vacation, relaxing, sleeping, exercising, shopping, cooking, hanging out, watching sports, and everything else one does that makes life worth living.

While billable time and hitting your hours is essential to a successful Biglaw career, so too is making the time for other things in life. This chapter is all about making the room in your schedule for unbillable time. How do you keep some semblance of a normal life when Biglaw demands so much of your time? It's not always easy, but it can be done.

You might be wondering, is this work-life balance? In an ideal world, we would all live lives with the perfect balance between the amount of time we spend at work and the amount of time we spend outside of it. For Biglaw associates, that's the balance among billable, non-billable, and unbillable time, and achieving a perfect balance is somewhat unrealistic. Instead, a better goal for Biglaw associates is to lead lives where one aspect (work) doesn't dominate the rest, causing everything else to be pushed to the side.

How Can Biglaw Associates Lead Full Lives?

It is possible to hit your required billable hours and still have a life outside of the office. It is up to all Biglaw associates to create boundaries between work and other aspects of their lives. Otherwise, the work part of life will creep into the parts of life supposedly reserved for other things (for unbillable time). For a Biglaw associate, work may creep in when you can't stop obsessively checking and responding to work emails on the weekends. Maybe you keep a running work to-do list in the back of your mind at all times. None of this is billable time, but it is interfering with and creeping into your precious unbillable time.

One of the biggest challenges about working in Biglaw is managing your time because work can pop up at almost any moment. Even partners are at the beck and call of their clients (with a little bit more room for pushback). Associates are at the beck and call of their clients *and* the partners they work for, so you never know when someone is going to ask you to do something.

If you can set a boundary between work and home and essentially "turn off" your brain with respect to work when you are actually off the clock, you will be able to recharge much better than the person in the office next to yours who might work the same number of hours, but who feels like she spends more time working because she is always thinking about work.

Here are some ways to manage your time so you can fill your schedule with enough unbillable time to make your billable time and the hours devoted to Biglaw worth it.

1. Be Selective With What Hobbies, Interests, and Personal Obligations You Keep

Unfortunately, there won't be time for everything you want to do.

But if you choose wisely, you'll have time for what matters most. Take stock of what your current hobbies, interests, and personal obligations are so you can evaluate what must stay and what you can give up. With only so many hours in a day, Biglaw associates have to make some hard choices when it comes to their personal lives.

The first step is to think of and write down everything outside of your job that you participate in now (e.g., taking care of children, going to a weekly soccer game, having a monthly dinner with friends, learning a new language, reading novels, playing video games) and write it down, along with an estimate of how much time each takes, whether that is daily, weekly, monthly, etc. Parents and other caregivers will have more limited time to devote to other things, but there is still space, albeit small, for other interests. Is there anything you wish you had more time for (e.g., training for a marathon, learning to cook vegan food, spending more time with your partner)? If so, write that down, too, along with an estimate of how much time you'll need to devote to it.

After reading through your list, it's time to make some cuts. What *must* you continue doing? What can you cut out? What would you like to add? What would be nice but isn't essential? Based on your answers, let go (at least temporarily) of what is not the most important to you and don't feel guilty about it. Just get rid of it, from your house and from your mind, and use your precious free time and mental energy to do what you love. With a clear picture of what obligations you have and what matters to you, you will not waste time on other things, which will clear up some time in your schedule.

2. Put Your Personal Commitments Into Your Work Calendar

In the last chapter, we talked about blocking your calendar off for time to get your work done. You should also add your personal commitments to your work calendar. Even if they take place after traditional business hours (there is no real concept of "after hours" in Biglaw, anyway), add your personal commitments to your work calendar.

Treat these as obligations and do everything in your power to make them happen. If you share your calendar with others on your team, putting your commitments into the calendar will be helpful to them, too, for planning purposes. If they see that you have time blocked off from 7:00 p.m. to 10:00 p.m. on Wednesday, they will hopefully take note of that and respect it. Of course, this isn't guaranteed, but it is helpful, and if you do the same for your colleagues when they schedule things into their calendars, they will likely do the same for you.

3. Don't Stop Making Plans Because You Might Have to Cancel Them

As a Biglaw associate, you will have to make sacrifices in your personal life because you won't be able to make it to everything you want, but don't give up trying. Things always come up last minute in Biglaw, and you will have to bail on your commitments sometimes, but don't let this possibility stop you from ever making plans.

It starts out slowly. Maybe you stop agreeing to a Friday happy hour with your friends because your schedule is unpredictable. It's easier to pass on drinks in the first place than to disappoint your friends yet again by bailing at the last minute. Sooner or later, you might be left off of the drinks invite list altogether. Once this starts to happen, you've given up. With this attitude, everything you are thinking and projecting will surely come true: you will miss those drinks.

When I was at my firm, I slowly stopped planning to do things during the week. It was easier not to put something on the calendar than to cancel on something or feel stressed out about "escaping" from the office at 7:00 p.m. to make it to dinner. The weekends were way easier to plan things during, but when you stop planning things or accepting invitations, those invitations eventually dwindle (even on the weekends). I regret that I let this happen because it doesn't have to.

There is always work to do, and if you expect to be in the office for twelve or more hours a day, the work will usually be there to fill the time. Somehow, you'll manage to fill your days and nights with something firm-related. Make a commitment to yourself early on in your career that you are not going to let this happen.

4. Share Your Interests With Your Team So They Know What's Important to You

Sharing parts of your personal life with your team, especially those with whom you work very closely, is central to keeping yourself sane and not losing yourself on the job. It is also important when it comes to flexibility and being able to take time off. We talked about this in *Chapter Eighteen*, but it's important enough to reiterate here.

If you take the time to get to know your coworkers and let them in so they get to know you, over time, you'll gain an understanding of what is meaningful to everyone. You'll know what exercise classes they like to take, what their husbands do for a living, what they do on the weekends, and what activities their kids participate in. As you gain more insight into their lives, and they into yours, you will develop a relationship that goes beyond just working together. You'll get to know each other on a personal level and they will be much more likely to understand and respect your commitments outside of the office. This way, when you have something personal to go to, they will understand and respect your commitments.

5. Maintain Friendships Outside of Biglaw

Most people have plenty of friends going into Biglaw, but the key is to keep them once you've started the job. It can be challenging to maintain friendships, either because your friends have more time than you do and don't understand why you're never able to hang out or why you cancel plans all of the time, or because your friends are in Biglaw, too, so they are just as busy as you are.

If you are the type of person who works hard to keep in touch with people, you'll be the kind of person who keeps friendships while in Biglaw. If you are used to people planning around you, inviting you to things, and reaching out to you, you might find that your friendships fade away.

Make an effort to keep your friendships with non-Biglaw associates. They will push you to make and keep plans, will encourage you to do things outside of work, and will remind you that there is life outside of Biglaw. If a junior banker, a resident doctor, or a school principal can all make time for a monthly dinner, why can't you?

6. Outsource What You Can

Despite large student loan balances, many Biglaw associates are fortunate enough to be in the financial position to outsource many of their everyday tasks. The number of daily tasks that you can outsource is not only mind-boggling, in particular in large cities such as New York, but is also growing by the day.

Someone can pick up, wash, fold, and drop off your laundry. Your groceries can magically appear at your doorstep and your dog can be walked three times a day, all while you're busy at work. Someone can even come to your apartment to give you a massage or a personal training session, and the list goes on and on. Some law firms offer outsourcing help right at the office, such as connecting you with a concierge who can book your medical appointments, a travel consultant who can help book a personal vacation, and a shoeshine who walks around the office shining shoes right outside your door while you continue to work.

You should definitely take advantage of these offerings. If you hate to clean, by all means, hire someone to come once a week and turn your apartment into a sparkly haven so you can spend the weekend doing something that lights you up. But be careful not to outsource *everything*. Some of these routine, normal activities make you feel productive, happy, fulfilled, and part of society! Before you know it, if you outsource too much, someone else is doing everything for you. For some people, this might be a good thing, but many will miss the normalcy of doing certain daily activities.

If you start to outsource things you love just because you can – such as cooking or walking your dog – to make time for Biglaw, that's a problem. If you choose to outsource them to make time for something you love more (like being with your children), that's OK. It's a personal choice. Just because you can outsource something does not mean that you have to, or that you have to do it every week. Ultimately, it's about learning the balance between outsourcing what will truly help you and make your life easier and outsourcing the things you wish you were doing yourself, but can't because Biglaw is interfering with too much of your life.

7. Be Flexible

The uncertainty of when work might come in for a junior associate makes it challenging to plan your life outside of work. This is why being flexible about when you can squeeze in your outside interests, obligations, and tasks is so vital. Here are a few suggestions on how you can be flexible and fit in the time for your unbillable interests:

- Go to the gym or for a run in the park at lunchtime, during a lull in work, or after business hours.
- Come to the office a few hours late if you know you'll be working late that night. Get some things done, like grocery shopping, before work in the late morning.
- Run an errand in the middle of the day during a slow period. Book your doctor's appointments during business hours when people in most other industries can't leave work (without taking time off).

8. Anticipate Conflicts and Work Around Them

While flexibility can help, it can only take you so far, as you can't always move everything. For example, if you play in a weekly softball league, your game time is not up to you. Does this mean you can't play softball? Maybe, but maybe not. Don't join a softball league with friends who are all teachers and where the games always begin at 5:00 p.m. Instead, join one that plays their games later in the evening or on the weekend, when it's more likely you'll be able to attend. Committing to something at 5:00 p.m. is setting yourself up for failure.

If you anticipate conflicts and avoid them ahead of time, the chances are higher that you'll be able to make your commitments. Push the non-negotiable things to the weekends. It's much more likely you won't have to bail on something on the weekend than on a Tuesday evening. Biglaw partners will assume that you will be at your desk (or at the very least available to work from home) on a weekday evening, but not on the weekend (without first giving you a heads-up).

9. Manage Your Expectations

Lastly, you must learn to manage your expectations. This is Biglaw, after all, so plans will be made, work will interfere, and plans will be missed. Do your part not to make plans that are unreasonable and, hopefully, you won't have to cancel too often.

~ ~ ~

Being a Biglaw associate is a huge part of your life, but it shouldn't be everything, even for the most devoted and exceptional associates (you!). Make sure you have enough unbillable time in life and carve out time away from work to enjoy that time. You're a Biglaw associate, but you're more than that.

Ask yourself: if you were to leave Biglaw tomorrow and your identity was no longer wrapped up in being "yourname@lawfirm.com," would you still have an identity? What would you tell people you were interested in? What are your hobbies? What do you do for fun? If there comes a time when you cannot answer these questions or separate yourself from your work persona, it might be time to reevaluate your situation. You want your Biglaw career to be a piece of your identity, not the entire pie.

Chapter Twenty-One

How to Be a Healthy Biglaw Lawyer

What it means to be "healthy" is different for everyone, but no matter what their definition is, many Biglaw lawyers don't come close to meeting it. Biglaw is a stressful place where client demands come above everything else, including the health of its lawyers. While this is changing somewhat and many Biglaw firms have implemented various wellness initiatives and spent huge amounts of money on these programs, Biglaw remains a stressful place where work comes first. Staying healthy can be especially challenging, but it can be done.

If you already have a strategy that feels good and works for you, the best thing you can do for your health is to stick with that while working in Biglaw. Pressure and time constraints will force you to give up some things, but if it is vital to your health, do everything in your power to stick with it.

If you need help developing some healthy habits for yourself as you enter Biglaw or if you are an associate struggling with your health, here are a few tips to get you started. None of these are earth shatteringly innovative, and you've undoubtedly heard some variation of them before, but it never hurts to be reminded to put your health first. You won't always hear that message coming from within Biglaw.

Diet and Exercise

When it comes to exercise, squeezing in the time to get it done is tough for everyone. That's especially true for Biglaw lawyers where there never seems to be time for anything but work. Make it a point to work out, if that's something you like to do, even if it takes some trial and error to figure out when you can fit it in. You will have to prepare ahead of time and be flexible when it comes to finding the time. Maybe that means being open to going for a run in the middle of the day (instead of when you'd prefer to do it early in the evening) or during a lull at work if you know you'll be at the office until late into the night. It's OK to be unavailable for an hour or so to take a walk, go for a run, or make it to a gym class, so long as you let your team know when you'll be back and you don't leave in the middle of a fire drill.

Sometimes you don't even have to go anywhere to get to the gym; it will be right in your office. Many firms have their own gyms that are free for associates to use and equipped with everything you'd need to work out, including fancy Peloton bikes and extra workout clothes if you forget yours at home (my firm's offerings were super unflattering, but hey, they did the trick in a pinch!). Don't be too embarrassed or shy (like I was for many years) to use the firm's gym. Get over yourself: everyone else is too preoccupied with himself or herself to notice you.

It's even easier to eat healthy than to work out when working in Biglaw. You might be surprised to hear that, but it's true. The only barrier you'll be up against when it comes to eating healthy is your own willpower and decision-making, because whatever you want to eat will be at your fingertips at all times.

Whatever a healthy diet is for you, make it easy on yourself to stick with that healthy diet, no matter what. Keep healthy breakfast bars and snacks around in case you are too busy to step out for lunch. Try to avoid the catered, greasy lunches and fatty sandwiches that always seem to be available at the firm. Free snacks that are always lying around aren't going to do you any favors, either. For dinners spent at your desk, where you will be relying on delivery from a website like Seamless, find a restaurant or two and a few healthy go-to orders. It'll make it easier not to be tempted to order something greasy with a side of fries and a coke. Left to our own devices, especially in times of stress or lack of sleep, most of us will succumb to making poor food choices. If you can eliminate the bad options and replace them with healthy choices, you'll be a much healthier Biglaw associate.

Drinking at Cocktail Parties, Happy Hours, and Other Events

From firm cocktail parties to happy hours with your coworkers to client dinners, there is no shortage of opportunities to drink when you are a Biglaw associate. During the summer, when summer associates descend on the firm and it's basically the firm's mission and associates' second jobs to show summer associates a good time, there are even more chances to drink.

These events can be tons of fun and, if you enjoy drinking, you'll enjoy the unlimited (and free) alcohol that is poured at all of them. I'm not going to suggest how much you should or should not drink since that's a personal decision, but I will tell you that nobody cares if you *don't* drink, so you should never feel pressured to. It should always be a choice and you should never feel pressured "for your career" to drink.

If you are feeling burned out or exhausted from going to yet another firm social event, it's OK to skip them from time to time. However, choose wisely which ones you go to and which ones you skip. Should you skip the cocktail hour hosted by the firm's chairman? Definitely not. Can you skip the summer associate party at a bowling alley? Definitely yes. Even when you do attend a cocktail party or another event where alcohol is served, nobody cares what's in your glass. Alcohol is a big part of Biglaw culture, but it doesn't have to be a big part of *your* Biglaw experience if you don't want it to be.

Don't Skip Your Appointments

Busy Biglaw lawyers tend to let non-work things fall by the wayside. It can be easy to put something like a doctor's appointment off for an extended period of time because you are just "too busy" to get to it. Biglaw is actually a lousy excuse for missing these appointments for a few reasons.

First, many Biglaw firms have on-site health centers. You can get minor things, like a sinus infection or a prescription refill, taken care of without ever having to leave the building. Not every firm has this, but if your does, it's a great perk.

Second, and this applies to everyone, is that Biglaw offers more flexibility than most traditional workplaces. When it comes to time devoted to the job and the amount of time you must be available for it, Biglaw is demanding. But when it comes to the ability to leave the office at 2:00 p.m. to make a doctor's appointment or work from home for the day, Biglaw is one of the best places to work. Take advantage of that flexibility and keep up with any health-related appointments you need to keep yourself at your healthiest.

Don't Forget About Your Mental Health

Your mental health is just as important (if not more) as your physical health is to your success as a Biglaw associate. Your mind is your ultimate asset as a lawyer, so keeping it sharp and in tip-top shape should be at the top of your to-do list.

Biglaw can get stressful. You're going to feel stretched, challenged, confused, and uncomfortable at times, but if you have the tools to deal with it, it won't always overwhelm you. Having a strategy to calm yourself down when your stress levels and blood pressure are rising through the roof will be extremely beneficial to your overall health. Whatever you currently do to keep yourself sane, keep it up, and we'll talk more specifically about stress in Biglaw, and how to deal with it, in the next chapter.

Keep Your Self-Esteem Intact

At times, Biglaw may beat you down and make you question whether you are smart enough, good enough, dedicated enough, or whatever your version of that question is, to be there. Are you *enough*? Of course you are. If any of these feelings of doubt creep in, you are experiencing a classic case of imposter syndrome. The good news is that everyone gets it, even Biglaw partners. The bad news is that everyone gets it, even Biglaw partners, which means it is not something that automatically goes away as you advance in your career. The little voice inside that tells you that you don't belong or aren't good enough to be there does, however, start to fade away, so long as you acknowledge its presence and fight back.

Remember how we talked about making mistakes? That sometimes you will make dumb mistakes, sometimes your mistakes will be the product of the fact that you are working at an incredible pace for an astonishing number of hours in a row, with little time to sleep, and that sometimes mistakes will just happen because we are all human and that's what we do. Unfortunately, because your clients expect perfection, when it is not produced, you will probably hear about it, sometimes in an unpleasant way. This is when your imposter syndrome is likely to pop up and say "Hi." And it's why it is so essential to combat your imposter syndrome and low self-esteem in Biglaw from the very beginning.

What can an associate do? Know that you may get put down, made to feel incompetent, and yelled at (rarely), but remember that you are smart and deserve to be there. Aside from giving yourself a pep talk, there are other things you can do to keep your self-esteem high and push imposter syndrome aside.

I kept a folder in my email inbox with a copy of every compliment I received at work, no matter how small. Sometimes it was something big, like an email from a client saying the transaction was a huge success and thanking me for my hard work. These went right into the folder. So, too, did the one-off "great job, kid" email from an older partner or the "you are a life-saver" email from a junior banking client. This folder will serve as a resource for you to look to whenever you have a low moment and are wondering if you ever should have gone to law school in the first place. Going back over those compliments can give you the little boost you need to remind yourself that there are partners at the firm who think you deserve to be there and clients who rely on you, both of whom would have been lost in certain moments without your help.

Similar to the folder of compliments, I also found value in saving the official firm reviews I received, especially the "upward reviews" given by more junior associates. Even if a client did not appreciate my work or I felt like I was not doing a good enough job, if I reminded myself that my coworkers thought I was valuable and could prove that to myself with real evidence by re-reading a review someone had written about me, I was able to push through even the most difficult situations.

Always remember that if you are giving 100% of your effort to your job, you are doing enough. You will make mistakes and get reprimanded for those mistakes, and your self-esteem might take a hit. If you can learn to move on quickly, not take things said during stressful situations personally, and remind yourself as often as you can that you are intelligent, capable, hard-working, and deserve to be there, you will succeed in Biglaw. Whenever you need some evidence of that, click through your "compliment" folder and past reviews and remember the times where you kicked butt and were recognized for it.

Ask for Help If You Need It

You are never alone in Biglaw, even if it feels like that at times. To stay healthy in Biglaw, you have to open up to your colleagues, family, and friends and ask for help when you need it.

Biglaw culture prides itself on sacrifice, powering through tough situations with little sleep (sometimes for days on end) to get things done, and putting work above everything else. It is a badge of honor to stay at the office all night or work all weekend. Because of this culture, you might feel like you can't ask for help when you are struggling, because it could be seen as a sign of weakness. I encourage lawyers to not only ask for help when they need it, but to offer it and make themselves someone at the firm that other lawyers can feel comfortable confiding in.

If you are feeling overwhelmed with an assignment or feeling too much pressure leading a project on your own, tell someone on your team how you feel. You won't do your best work under those circumstances, so suffering through it won't benefit anyone. If you are struggling with work or something else in your life, there is an extensive support network of people within the firm that you can turn to, such as the HR department or the associate development team, in addition to your direct coworkers. There are support networks outside of the firm, too, that you can tap into for help before you reach a breaking point. Your health is more important than Biglaw.

~ ~ ~

If you want to work in Biglaw for an extended period of time, you have to take care of yourself. Take time for yourself to make sure your physical and mental health do not fall by the wayside in exchange for more billable hours. In the end, an unhealthy lawyer is not valuable to the firm, either. It's in your best interests and the firm's to stay healthy. Biglaw is an intense place, but it's not without compassion. Only when you open up and talk to someone can you get the help you need.

Chapter Twenty-Two

Signs and Symptoms of Biglaw Burnout

The culture of Biglaw sets up the perfect storm for associate burnout. "Work hard, play hard" probably sounds familiar to high-achieving Biglaw associates and law students. It's a motto most have lived with even before reaching Biglaw and it can be a dangerous one. Toughing it out, powering through late nights, burning the candle at both ends, staying at the office overnight, drinking caffeine at all hours of the day to keep you going, and eating meals at your desk are all looked upon favorably in Biglaw. After your first all-nighter in Biglaw, you might feel a sense of pride or accomplishment, like you've been initiated into some secret club. However good that club is for your career, it can be detrimental to your health and lead to burnout.

Another factor inherent in Biglaw that leads to burnout is the perfectionism expected by its clients, partners, and Biglaw associates themselves. Anything short of perfection, including the need to take a break once in a while to, you know, get some sleep, is seen as a weakness.

What Is Burnout?

What does all of this non-stop work and chronic stress lead to? If left unmanaged, no time to rest, no resources to alleviate the burden, and demands that are too high for a person to consistently meet, will lead to burnout. Burnout is a state of mental, emotional, and physical exhaustion.

Slowly but surely, burnout may creep into a Biglaw associate's life. You might not see it approaching until it's already too late. Unless you are on notice of the signs and symptoms, that is. Once someone reaches the point of burnout, they will no longer find meaning in their work. It will all seem pointless. The World Health Organization (WHO) includes burnout in its International Classification of Diseases and recognizes it as an "occupational syndrome." They define it as "chronic workplace stress that has not been successfully managed," which is characterized by "feelings of energy depletion or exhaustion; increased mental distance from one's job, or feelings of negativism or cynicism related to one's job; and reduced professional efficacy."

What Is It About Biglaw, Specifically, That Leads to High Rates of Burnout?

There is no such thing as "easing into" Biglaw. After a few days of training, you will be staffed on an assignment. And just like that, you will have become someone's lawyer. And that someone is a client who expects perfection and who is paying a lot of money for you to work as efficiently and as quickly as possible.

The pressure in Biglaw is high, the work is demanding, and there is a steep learning curve. This can result in an especially high rate of burnout among Biglaw associates. The reasons below, whether alone or combined, can lead to burnout in a Biglaw associate. Watch out for when:

1. You have too much work on your plate and are overwhelmed with trying to get it all done.
2. You don't take enough breaks. You eat all of your meals at your desk, never take walks, and never take a moment to call your family.
3. You put too much pressure and too many expectations on yourself.
4. You feel a constant level of stress, punctuated by times of extreme stress when a crisis hits.
5. You don't have enough support; whether it is a lack of junior associate support, paralegal support, or partner support, you are left hanging to deal with too many things on your own.
6. You don't get enough sleep, which leads to chronic fatigue.
7. You take ownership of not only your own work but of others' work, and you carry the bulk of the team on your back, even when others should be taking ownership of their parts. You feel responsible for everything.
8. You miss meaningful personal events and feel not only sad about missing them but guilty about it.
9. You have responsibilities outside of work that you feel you are dropping the ball on because you don't have any time to devote to them.

10. You feel like you can never say "no" to an assignment, even if you physically cannot take on one more minute of work (for more on how to say "no," and when you can and should, even in Biglaw, see *Chapter Nineteen*).

11. You feel like you don't have any control over your work. Your schedule, workload, and timing of all that you do are dictated by someone else.

How to Recognize Burnout in Biglaw: Common Signs and Symptoms

Now that you know some of the factors that lead to burnout, how exactly does burnout manifest itself? Every person will react differently to the same circumstances, so one person who experiences some or many of the factors above may never reach the point of burnout. In contrast, another person may reach that point quite early on in their career with just a few of the common factors present. Once you have reached the point of burnout, these are some signs and symptoms you will likely experience:

1. Chronic Exhaustion: no matter how much you rest or sleep, you are exhausted. Chronic fatigue cannot be cured by taking a short vacation or catching up on lost sleep over the weekend.

2. Feeling Ineffective: no matter how much effort you put in or how much time you spend at work, you feel as though you aren't progressing or getting anything done.

3. Cynicism: you feel cynical about your job, about your life outside of work, and even about things you used to take pride and joy in. You have a general sense of disengagement from

work and from life.

4. Inability to Focus: you cannot focus and your attention span has decreased. You can't concentrate, your productivity drops, and you might be performing poorly or producing lower quality work.

5. Physical Symptoms: burnout manifests itself not only in the emotional and mental, but in the physical as well. You might get sick more often, have frequent headaches, digestive issues, difficulty sleeping, or tightness in the chest.

6. Other Signs: other signs include an increased desire to be alone, absenteeism from the job, social withdrawal, anger, forgetfulness, anxiety, panic attacks, pessimism, and irritability.

As you can probably tell from these signs and symptoms, burnout makes it almost impossible to be an effective and productive associate, which means burnout is a problem both for the associate who experiences it and also for the firm. Not only that, but burnout also tends to hit those associates who are the most dedicated to the firm; the ones who devote their entire lives to work, consistently work late, go above and beyond what is asked of them, and strive for perfection. While these are great attributes for the firm, those same attributes can be detrimental when an associate reaches his breaking point. Law firms are incentivized to keep their lawyers healthy and at the top of their games, and have taken steps in recent years to address the sometimes unhealthy demands placed on their lawyers. However, the success of these efforts varies significantly by firm, so it is ultimately up to you to take care of yourself.

Recognizing Burnout in Your Coworkers

While it is up to you to recognize when you are on the path to burnout and to do something about it, sometimes that is easier said than done. Burnout can creep in and go unnoticed as the changes in you take place slowly. You likely won't wake up one day, suddenly burned out, when you were completely fine the day before. It might be up to others to help you recognize burnout in yourself, and it might be up to you to recognize it in your colleagues.

A good law firm associate is always available to his colleagues and his clients, pulls his own weight on the team, and provides excellent legal advice. An excellent associate goes above and beyond this: he not only looks out for the firm's partners and clients by providing top-notch legal services, but he also looks out for his own health and for the health of his colleagues.

Biglaw, like so many jobs, takes up so many hours of a person's day. If you take a step back and look at your waking hours, you are very likely to spend more time with your coworkers than with your family and friends, even those family members that you live with. This means that even though Biglaw coworkers aren't technically your family, you owe it to them to look out for their health, too. This can be a tricky line to toe. How do you interject about something as personal as someone's health, when they aren't truly your family? Awkward as it may be, it is essential to do. Familiarize yourself with the signs and symptoms of burnout, not only for yourself, but for your Biglaw family members, too.

In recent years, there have been some high-profile cases of Biglaw burnout that have had tragic endings. From partner suicides to death by exhaustion, Biglaw has been in the headlines for all of the wrong reasons. How did family members miss the signs, people wonder? What could have been done to prevent these tragedies? Nothing can be done to bring back those we lost, but we can help those who are struggling and still in Biglaw. While burnout does not necessarily lead to horrible consequences like suicide, it certainly can lead a person down an unpleasant path and exacerbate underlying mental health conditions.

What can Biglaw lawyers do about it? There are so many little things that signal burnout – a consistently closed door, a change in personality or sense of humor – that we as colleagues can notice about our Biglaw family members that their actual family can't see because they just don't spend as much time with their loved ones as we do. As healthy lawyers, we owe it to our colleagues and their families to make sure we take care of ourselves and each other. If you see something amiss in the mental health of a colleague, reach out and check in to see what you can do to help.

~ ~ ~

Hopefully, you'll never reach the point of burnout. But you should understand why Biglaw is the perfect breeding ground for burnout, and learn the signs and symptoms. Even if you don't face it yourself, you're bound to have a coworker who does. Know how to recognize it so you can offer a hand. Nobody should suffer from Biglaw burnout alone.

Chapter Twenty-Three

How to Prevent Burnout and What to Do If You Get Burned Out

How you handle stress, which, if handled poorly, can ultimately lead to burnout, might very well determine whether or not you will survive and succeed in Biglaw. While things on the surface may seem calm (save for that lone partner who can be heard down the hallway screaming over the phone at opposing counsel), the underlying vibe of many Biglaw offices is quite the opposite.

Everything needs to be done ASAP or yesterday, redone, fixed, distributed before anyone can go to sleep, filed in court by the 5:00 p.m. deadline, sent to your client before he jets off on vacation and is unreachable for ten days, and the list goes on and on. Switch out the business casual wardrobe for scrubs and Biglaw offices might as well be the emergency rooms of the corporate world. Who do the emergency room levels of tension and stress hit? They hit the junior associates, hard.

In addition to being thrown into the Biglaw world with relatively little preparation, work can be particularly challenging for junior associates because what needs to get done in a time crunch often falls to the junior members of the team. A task like making sure an original note arrives at the Trustee's office in time for an 8:00 a.m. closing, while not something that requires a law degree, has the likelihood of causing an enormous amount of stress for a junior associate.

Let's take our note delivery, for example. In theory, that note just needs to make it to an office downtown. But did you realize that the note was being held in a vault at the client's offices in Buffalo, New York, not in Manhattan, there is a winter storm brewing, and neither UPS, FedEx nor DHL will resume deliveries from Buffalo to New York City until after your closing will have taken place? This exact situation happened to me as a junior associate. While the details of how we figured it out are not important, the paralegal and I on the deal did manage to get the note to where it needed to be just in time for closing. Our stress levels were at about an eleven that day.

Tasks like the one I just described are often the most stressful because clients assume you can make miracles happen, and at the hundreds or thousands of dollars an hour they pay, they expect just that. What can you do to keep your stress levels down and prevent burnout when everything you do seems to be treated like a life or death situation? Fortunately, there are ways.

How to Prevent Burnout and Cope With the Stresses of Biglaw

Once burnout hits, it can be hard (although not impossible) to overcome without making some drastic changes. It's better to prevent burnout than to try to treat it (more on that below). Here's what you can do.

1. Take Care of Yourself

Preventing burnout starts with being a healthy lawyer. All of the habits of healthy lawyers that we discussed in *Chapter Twenty-One*, such as the importance of regular exercise, meditation, sleep, eating healthy, listening to your body when it is warning you of overwork, recharging, taking time away from the office, and generally making your health a priority, apply.

There are other ways to support your mental health while dealing with a stressful Biglaw life. De-stressing for you might mean closing your door and taking a few minutes to yourself before calling a client back, putting on headphones and zoning out, going for a walk alone, or finding a quiet, abandoned office to get some work done in peace. While these healthy habits and self-care acts alone cannot prevent burnout, they are a good place to start and come back to when things feel out of control.

2. Delegate, Delegate, Delegate and Use All of the Firm's Resources

No matter how junior you are, there is always someone at the firm you can delegate work to, whether it is a paralegal, summer associate, or the word processing department. Delegation is a skill you need to develop and practice, so start to get comfortable with it early on in your career. As you become more senior, you will not be able to survive Biglaw without significant delegation. You must trust your team members and not try to do it all yourself. Beginning when you are a junior associate, use all of the resources your firm has to offer to your advantage. Get the help and support that you need. Do you need updated technology? Ask for it. Do you need another person on the deal? Ask for one. You might be told "no," but you will often be told "yes," and every little thing that helps save you time can alleviate some of your burden and leaves more time for non-work and non-stressful things in your life.

3. Speak Up for Yourself and Learn How to Say "No"

You are the only one who knows how much work you have. If you are swamped with work and given an additional assignment that will put you over the edge, speak up and (diplomatically) say "no" (for more on how to do this the right way, see *Chapter Nineteen*). Explain what you have on your plate and let the assigning attorney know that you will not be able to complete the assignment by the deadline, given what you already have to work on. It's in his best interests, too, that you produce quality work, so he will usually be grateful that you were upfront about your availability as opposed to turning in a poor quality work product (or none at all).

If you can take on a new assignment when you are very busy, set clear boundaries with the attorneys on your team as to your availability and your time constraints because of other work. One small assignment can sometimes morph into a giant one in Biglaw, so set your boundaries early on. Being a junior associate doesn't mean you have to be a doormat.

4. Quickly Move on From Your Mistakes and Stop Expecting Perfection

When you make a mistake, do what you need to do to make it right and move on. Instead of dwelling on an error, which will only increase your stress levels, learn from it so you don't repeat it in the future, but don't beat yourself up over it. Along the same lines, stop expecting perfection out of yourself. That way, when you inevitably do make a mistake, the consequences won't feel like such a personal blow.

5. Don't Compare Yourself to Other Associates and Don't Compete With Them

Whether you are making comparisons based on what deals you are staffed on, who others are working with, or, the most straightforward metric to use for comparison purposes – how many hours everyone is working – don't fall into the comparison trap. Your career is your own and while it is true that you're competing with other associates for work and for partner attention, the best way to succeed is to put your head down and do your absolute best work.

In fact, everyone works differently, so it is impossible to compare yourself, especially if you are comparing billable hours or time spent in the office. There will be some associates who spend fourteen hours a day, no matter what, in the office. They are either working on a busy matter or they are not that efficient, you just never know. Biglaw associates can't compare themselves to others based on the number of hours worked, so don't even try to do it.

Yes, Biglaw is sort of a competition. Everyone can't get the best work or the best assignments, and everyone can't bill the most hours or be the partner's favorite, but there is room for everyone. By the time partnership rolls around, most associates will have left. The competition essentially eliminates itself. The best way to get ahead is to do your best work, focus on yourself, and not worry about what others are working on or how much others are billing.

6. Keep Your "Therapy" Appointments (Whatever They May Be for You)

If you attend weekly therapy sessions with a doctor, make that appointment a non-negotiable. There are other forms of therapy, too, that you should keep. Maybe running is your form of "therapy;" if so, don't skip your daily run for too many days in a row. Perhaps you already have a meditation practice or something else that helps keep you sane and grounded. If so, don't allow the "busy-ness" of Biglaw to let those things drop out of your daily routine.

7. Pinpoint What (Or Who) Stresses You Out

It is important to identify what it is about the job that is stressful. Maybe what stresses you out is the general atmosphere and vibe of a particular group. Some partners and associates thrive in a high-energy, constantly "on" environment (not to stereotype, but you can usually find these people in the M&A group). If you cannot handle the constant barrage of "emergencies" that come with working with people and on deals like that, then you should find another group to work with.

There are plenty of people in Biglaw who can handle stress and who are even-keeled almost all of the time: seek them out. They will bring you down (in a good way) and ease your tension. Others handle stress by tensing up and looking like they are about to cry at the drop of a hat. Do not work for these associates! By managing who you work with, you can lower your stress levels and maintain your sanity.

8. Be a Calming Presence for Those Around You

When you become a mid-level and senior associate, you can use your position of influence to create a sense of calm across your whole team. When a junior associate frantically rushes into your office, rambling about a missing signature page, be the best teammate you can be by simply not freaking out.

Remind yourself and your colleague that while this must be fixed as soon as possible, it is going to work out. A calm presence in the office is one of the most valuable assets you can bring to a team. When there's a constant level of stress, working with someone who is even-keeled and calm, even in times of high-pressure and high-stress, is refreshing. A calm presence helps not only your colleagues, but it helps yourself, too. By de-escalating a situation and calming the whole room down, you help calm yourself, too.

What If the Stress Never Goes Away? What to Do When You're Burned Out

Sleep, mindfulness, exercise, eating healthy – all of these things are great tools, but they alone cannot fix burnout once it has set in. What are you supposed to do if you feel stressed out all of the time, have panic attacks at work, and feel a deep sense of anxiety and helplessness?

It's normal to feel anxious about an upcoming work deadline once in a while, but when that anxiety becomes a weekly or daily pattern, it is something to worry about. A Biglaw career is not for everyone, and your health is more important than "making it" in Biglaw or pushing on just because it is what you are "supposed" to do. Biglaw stress doesn't have to lead to burnout, but sometimes it does. Here are a few things you can do if you think you've reached the point of burnout, or are almost there.

1. Seek Support

The most important thing to do is to seek support. Don't try to push through or go it alone. Biglaw culture traditionally values soldiering through a problem and figuring it out alone, but that can't be the attitude you take when it comes to your health.

Whether it is a coworker, family member, friend, law school classmate, or medical professional, start by talking with someone, anyone, if you are experiencing burnout. From there, you can begin to build your network of support and seek out more people who can offer help and guidance. This is a time when you need your support network more than ever, so don't be ashamed to ask for help.

It's important to note here that burnout and depression are not the same and shouldn't be treated the same way, but they do have some similar characteristics and are both prevalent in Biglaw lawyers. If you are struggling with either, or suspect you might be but aren't sure, talk to a healthcare professional and follow their advice.

2. Seek Meaning in Your Work

Sometimes changing how you view your work can help alleviate or reverse burnout. If you can't find meaning in what you are doing, can you reframe how you think about your clients and about the work you do for them? If you are representing a large corporation that you might not find meaning in representing, can you find meaning in helping the junior in-house counsel succeed at her job and accomplish your joint goals? Focus on your clients (the people themselves) and how critical your work is to them and how much they value you (even if they don't always show it).

You can also seek meaning by taking on more traditionally meaningful work: pro bono. Take on a case or take up an issue you care about. Think back to law school, why did you want to become a lawyer after all? There are endless ways to use your legal skills to give back, including in Biglaw. While taking on a new pro bono project probably won't solve your burnout problem, in the interim, it can give you a little boost of motivation and alleviate a bit of the feeling of burnout.

3. Explore Other Options Within the Firm

As a junior associate, you still have some wiggle room when it comes to transitioning from one practice group to another or from one sub-group to another. Talk to the assigning partners or your assignment coordinator and ask to explore a different practice area or ask to work with new people. Don't struggle in silence working for someone or on something you don't find any meaning in, especially if there is something else at the firm you think you'd like to try. It is worth giving something else a shot before giving up on Biglaw entirely.

Depending on your circumstances, you might have the option to pursue an alternative work arrangement, like a reduced schedule. While this is generally reserved for more senior associates who have proven their worth and can better manage a part-time schedule while still getting all of their required work done, it doesn't hurt to ask. If you have outside obligations or extenuating circumstances, the firm might be willing to be more flexible with you because of those.

Your firm might also offer an unpaid leave of absence. You can use the time to recharge and come back to the job refreshed or use the time away to decide what you want to do next. Many partners and associates have no idea what their firm's policy on taking a leave of absence is, so if that's something you're interested in, the best place to go for information is usually your firm's HR department.

4. Evaluate Your Exit Options

If you've tried these suggestions and none of them work, or you simply have to get out of Biglaw fast, evaluate your exit options and develop a plan. You want to leave Biglaw on a positive note, as you never know what connections you'll want to reach out to in the future, so don't leave abruptly or by burning any bridges.

Discuss your concerns with your mentors, sponsor (if you have one), partner supervisor, or any trusted authority figure at the firm and explain that you are burned out. There is no shame in burnout and law firms have seen it play out again and again. Remember that they, too, don't have much use for a burned out and unproductive associate, so it is in their best interests to help you transition out of Biglaw and find a place that is a better fit. If you know in your heart that it's time to leave, don't let anyone convince you otherwise. If it's time to go, it's time to go.

~ ~ ~

Biglaw is a demanding and stressful place for junior associates. For all lawyers, actually. At some point in your career, you may experience some of the telltale signs and symptoms of burnout. By taking preventative measures, some people can stop stress from turning into burnout, but not everyone can, no matter how much they try. If that is you, it's OK to acknowledge your burnout and take a step back, whether that means a change in the type of work you do, a temporary leave, a reduced schedule, or a full exit from Biglaw.

Chapter Twenty-Four

Why You Should Always Keep Your Resumé Current

The last time you prepared a resumé was probably during your 1L year of law school. For some, that was ages ago; for others, it wasn't that long ago; but for everyone, it was far enough back for your resumé to have become outdated. It served its purpose (to land you a Biglaw job) and you've probably never used it since, so it's time for an update.

Even if you are a recent law school graduate, if you've begun working as a lawyer, your old law school resumé is not as sophisticated or current as it should be. A practicing Biglaw attorney should have a resumé that includes information on key deals or cases she's worked on and should list out the tangible skills she's developed while on the job.

What follows are tips on how to update your resumé once you've begun working in Biglaw. In addition, there's an explanation as to *why* having a current and up-to-date resumé is so important, for everyone. If you are unhappy in Biglaw or at your current firm, the importance of having an updated resumé is obvious: to apply for new jobs. But even those associates who love their current firms and cannot imagine working anywhere else should periodically dust off their resumés and update them with any significant Biglaw accomplishments; you'll see why in this chapter.

How to Update Your Resumé

In law school, your career services office or law student peers were there to offer advice on how to craft your resumé to land a Biglaw job (or whatever your dream job was). As with many other things, once you leave school, you're now on your own to update your resumé. For many people, keeping your resumé current falls by the wayside. Here are some tangible ways you can update your resumé so it is always ready to use whenever the need arises.

1. Gather Information on Your Accomplishments as You Go

Your Biglaw accomplishments, be it a significant matter you worked on or an award you won, should make up the bulk of your resumé. Rather than relying on your memory to recollect everything you've worked on throughout your Biglaw career, get in the habit of filing away your accomplishments as they happen.

One way to do this is to gather information from firm announcements. Most firms send out an internal email or bulletin to the entire firm on a weekly or bi-weekly basis that details the various deals that just closed and the cases that recently went to trial or settled in a client's favor. Whenever a matter you worked on shows up in one of these announcements, save the blurb in a dedicated folder in your email box. This takes basically no time and creates a nice record of the projects you've worked on over the course of your career. The firm's emails are not very detailed, so, if time permits, make a few notes to yourself about the details of the project so you can remember it better in the future if you choose to include it on your resumé.

Taking it one step further, make some notes about what *you* specifically contributed to the project. For example, did you manage the diligence project for a massive, complex, multinational M&A deal? Write down all of the primary skills you used while handling that transaction. You might think you'll never be able to forget "Project X" aka "The Project From Hell That Consumed My Life for Three Months," but even if the memory of working an endless number of late nights is seared into your brain forever, you *will* forget the details and your specific contributions. It takes a surprisingly short amount of time to forget about the specific skills you learned while working on a project. For this reason, if you can write down your contributions to a project as soon as it ends, while everything is still fresh in your mind, that will serve you best.

While we're on the topic of including client-specific deals or cases on your resumé, this is a reminder that you should never include client names or identifying details unless the matter is public. A good rule of thumb for knowing when you can include client names or details on your resumé (or any non-confidential document) is to take a look at how the firm describes the matter. If your firm published details on its external website or in a lawyer's bio on the site, it's probably OK for you to do the same. Otherwise, stay on the safe side and refer to the client generally instead of by name or any identifying details (e.g., you should say "representation of a Fortune 500 pharmaceutical company" instead of "representation of Pfizer"). Following these guidelines will help you steer clear of violating any client confidentialities.

2. Track Your Progress Using the Firm's Benchmarks

In addition to tracking all of the firm's deals and cases you've worked on, you'll also want to track your developmental progress. Even after just a short amount of time in Biglaw, you will have acquired many skills – many more than you even realize.

How do you keep track of or even realize what skills you've picked up since starting your Biglaw career? The easiest way to do this is to refer to your firm's internal guidance as to where it expects associates to be and when. (For a more in-depth discussion on the benchmarks, see *Chapter Fifteen.*)

In addition to making sure you are on track for a long-term career at the firm, the benchmarks also serve for you to record what skills you have acquired. Take some time to review the skills expected of you at your level and pick out your strongest ones. These will be the ones you'll want to weave into your resumé when it comes time to update it.

3. Refer to Your Past Performance Reviews

Another great tool when it comes to updating your resumé is to refer to what other people have said about you and incorporate those positive comments into your resumé. Sometimes it is harder for us to realize good things about ourselves and it takes hearing them from another person to realize they are true. That is where performance reviews come into play.

After your first six months (or a year, depending on your firm's practices), you will have had at least one formal performance review and possibly more less-formal reviews, such as peer reviews. Save these reviews in a separate file for yourself because they will become valuable resources to refer back to as your career progresses and as you update your resumé.

Similar to how reviewing the firm benchmarks can jog your memory and make you aware of the skills you've developed, your performance reviews can serve to highlight which skills you are particularly strong in. Whatever the partners in your group and senior associates with whom you've worked have chosen to highlight as particular strengths of yours in your performance reviews are usually great attributes to add to your resumé.

4. Pull All of the Information You've Gathered to Update Your Resumé

If you keep track of your past deals, cases, and accomplishments, as well as the skills you've acquired, when it comes time to update your resumé, you will have all of the information you need right in front of you. Sit down one afternoon and pull the most relevant information from what you've gathered and work it into your resumé. You won't be able to include everything, as most guidance (with some exceptions) says to limit resumés to one page, but it is better to start with more information and cull it down to be sure you haven't missed anything notable.

Some lawyers also put together a "deal sheet" or a "case sheet," which is a separate document from their resumé listing the major matters they've worked on, along with a brief description of each and their role on it. It doesn't hurt to create one of these, too, especially if you've gathered all of the information anyway.

After you've updated your resumé with all of your Biglaw accomplishments, you'll probably feel very proud of yourself.

Sometimes, Biglaw can get you down and can make you feel as though you aren't doing anything right. Seeing how much you are learning and growing is an excellent way to remind yourself of all that you've accomplished and learned.

Why Should You Keep Your Resumé Current?

If you're hesitant to spend the time updating your resumé, hopefully, the following information changes your mind. Here's why it is so important.

1. Job Opportunities

- *For those who want to leave Biglaw:*

This one is pretty obvious: if you are unhappy at your job (either at your particular firm or with Biglaw in general), it's time to get out before you burn out. To land another job, you'll need an updated resumé. It's as simple as that.

- *For those who want to stay in Biglaw:*

What about those who are satisfied with their current jobs? Having an updated resumé is beneficial to you, too. What's the point of having a resumé if you don't plan to use it anytime soon?

No matter how satisfied you are at your current job, you never know when an even better opportunity will arise. There might be an opening for an in-house counsel position at one of your client's offices. If that client enjoys working with you so much, she might suggest that you interview for the position and it could turn out to be your dream job. Or maybe your best friend from college is hiring at his bank and wants you to send over your resumé so he can pass it on to his general counsel.

You never know what opportunities are out there, and if you don't have a resumé ready, you might miss out on any one of these chances. Job openings tend to pop-up quickly and get filled even quicker.

2. Other Opportunities

Traditionally used for job-searching, resumés are helpful tools to have for other reasons, too. These are just a few of many other ways an updated resumé can come in handy:

- *Non-Profit Boards:*

Many Biglaw lawyers do extensive pro bono work, devoting hours and hours of their time to specific legal services organizations. Whether it is for victims of domestic violence, immigrant detainees, or anything else, there are endless non-profit organizations that need the legal support of Biglaw attorneys. If you've found an organization you are devoted to, you might want to apply to be a member of that organization's board. This application process will undoubtedly require you to submit your resumé.

- *Your Firm Bio:*

Resumés are also helpful when you're crafting the bio that will appear alongside your picture on your firm's website and that is used to market you in various places. For example, if you accompany a partner to a pitch looking to land a new client, he will usually bring along the bios of all of the lawyers attending the pitch. Another use for your firm bio is when you attend conferences. If you attend a conference and would like to serve on a panel while there, having an updated resumé will come in handy when submitting your application for the panel.

- *Your Partnership "Application":*

Lastly, if the time comes for you to be put up for partner, you will actually need to "apply" for this new job, too. Even though your partnership "application" will very likely be submitted to your current firm, you will need to show the firm's partnership committee all that you've accomplished over the previous eight or so years. Of course, the partners with whom you work directly know the quality and breadth of your work, but the members of the partnership committee and the partnership as a whole, who will vote on whether or not you are elevated to partner, do not. It is your job to show them just how qualified you are.

By saving all of these matters you were a part of, the list of skills you've developed over the years (whether you put any of that into an official resumé form or not), and feedback you've received, you will have an easier time building your case for partnership. Not only will you have to spend less time trying to remember what it was you did over the last decade and 20,000 billable hours or so, but you will also be able to show a more fulsome history of all that you've accomplished and provide a stronger case for yourself.

~ ~ ~

Keeping your resumé current allows you to keep all of your options open. You never know when the perfect job or opportunity is going to fall into your lap or when you are going to decide that today is the last day you want to be a Biglaw attorney. Don't let not having a resumé stand in the way of any opportunity that might come your way.

Chapter Twenty-Five

Skills to Take With You If and When You Leave Biglaw

You're probably familiar with the old saying, "You can do anything with a law degree!" It's supposed to be comforting and encouraging to those entering the legal profession. Even if you don't really want to be a lawyer or don't think you want to be one forever, the saying suggests that a six-figure law degree is still a valuable investment. Many lawyers would disagree with the sentiment, as it can seem like there isn't anything we lawyers know how to do *but* practice law. Can you really do "anything" with a law degree?

Yes, you can! Lawyers aren't limited to practicing law. You can take the many skills that you acquire in your first couple of years of practicing Biglaw with you wherever you go and to whatever career you choose, whether it is within or outside of the law.

Statistically speaking, you are more likely to leave Biglaw as an associate than to stick around long enough to become a partner. The days when making partner was an attainable and realistic goal for many are long behind us. Nowadays, many people enter Biglaw not to one day make partner, but rather to pay off their student loans, gain valuable experience, and parlay that experience into an in-house legal job or one in another field entirely.

This last chapter is for those beginning their careers and questioning whether or not Biglaw is right for them. It's also for those who are in the midst of their careers, are struggling, and are wondering whether it's worth it to stay. And it's for those who, sometime during their Biglaw career, decide they want to leave but have no idea where they could possibly go. In-house at a bank sounds even worse than their current job and so does working at another firm. As they say, and a phrase that keeps many in Biglaw longer than they would like, "The Devil you know is better than the Devil you don't."

With just a couple of years of Biglaw under your belt, you will have gained many, many skills that you can take with you no matter where you decide to go next. Read on to see how these legal skills will be seen as considerable assets to potential employers in other legal and non-legal fields, too. Even if you're not thinking about leaving Biglaw, these are excellent reminders of all that Biglaw can teach you. I hope this encourages you and makes you realize that you really can do anything with a law degree (and even more with a Biglaw job on your resumé).

After working as a Biglaw associate, you will be able to:

1. Express Yourself Clearly and Concisely

Through writing countless emails, drafting legal briefs, preparing offering documents, and spending hours on the phone and in meetings, you will become an expert at expressing yourself clearly and concisely in a world where everyone wants the answer to a complex question quickly. Biglaw lawyers are experts at parsing through dense issues and presenting them to their clients in easily digestible formats. Not only will you have learned to get your point across clearly, but you'll also know how to be direct and get to the point.

2. Remain Calm Under Pressure

If you haven't gotten the memo yet, Biglaw is a stressful place. Working day-in and day-out in Biglaw means you will learn to rise above the stress and remain calm under the most trying circumstances. You'll learn not to let your feathers get ruffled at the first sign of any minor disruption or issue. It's hard to remain calm under pressure, but it's one of the first things you'll learn how to do in Biglaw.

3. Spot Issues

You'll learn to spot issues and problems better than anyone else. Not only will you be able to issue spot, but you will also be able to brainstorm solutions and solve complex problems, too. Being on the look-out for issues and spotting the things that others have missed is what makes a lawyer stand out, because the earlier you spot something, the sooner you can take care of it.

4. Meet Tight Deadlines

Biglaw is a high-paced, highly intense environment, with strict standards and tight deadlines. Not only does the work need to get done, but it also needs to be done well, no matter the circumstances. You will develop an ability to concentrate and get your work done even under the most extreme conditions. You will put your body through the wringer with all-nighters and sleepless weekends, but you'll make it out alive. If you can make it through a Biglaw all-nighter, a 300-plus billable hour month, or a daunting filing deadline, you can make it through anything.

5. Adapt to Anything and Anyone

In Biglaw, you'll run across some interesting and demanding partners and clients, with all kinds of working styles. You have to always be on your toes, ready for what will be thrown at you next, whether that is a new task or a new colleague. You'll learn to adapt to different working styles and learn to flow through corporate situations and life recognizing what people want and deliver what they need. Does a client need constant contact and updates, or does he prefer a short summary once a week and a phone call only when something is urgent? Does the partner you work for never read emails, or never answer his phone (or both, in which case your resourcefulness is going to come in handy)? All of these quirks and how you adapt to them will serve you well no matter where you end up working next.

6. Juggle Many Tasks at Once

Very rarely in Biglaw do you have only one matter that you're working on at a given time. Even within one matter, there will be many tasks to deal with. You'll become a master at juggling many tasks at once, prioritizing what needs to get done when, and making it happen. You'll be able to jump from one thing to the next, sometimes in a matter of minutes. You'll learn how to stay hyper-focused on the task at hand and then to switch to a new task, hardly losing a step along the way.

7. Have Top-Notch Organizational Skills

Even if you don't consider yourself an especially organized person before you begin your job, Biglaw will make you one. The sheer number of meetings, clients, matters, tasks, and commitments you have in Biglaw will force you to develop your own style of organization. Maybe it doesn't look pretty from the outside, but you'll come up with a system. By the time you leave Biglaw, you'll leave with top-notch organizational skills that can you can use to your advantage in any area of your life.

8. Work on and Lead Teams

While specific tasks themselves, like drafting a motion or a deal document, can be very solitary, Biglaw, in general, is very collaborative and involves working on a team with many other lawyers. After you've spent some time on the job, you will know how to lead teams and will have learned how to coordinate large cases and transactions with lots of moving pieces.

9. Delegate Tasks to Others

You will learn how to delegate tasks to everyone from more junior associates, to document services, and even (tactfully, and avoiding the pitfalls of "delegating up") to senior associates and partners. Having great delegation skills will free up your own time to pursue other work or tasks on your plate, and even give you more time outside of the office, which is something you can't put a price on, no matter where you end up next.

10. Manage Projects

Whether it is with a team of junior associates, your pro bono immigration client, the new paralegal, or your boss, you will become a master of project management after only a short time in Biglaw. While technical legal details and negotiations might be left to more senior associates, it will be your sole responsibility as a junior associate to ensure that all of the details are in place. Your ability to manage a large team, demanding clients, hundreds (or sometimes thousands) of documents, and a tight time-line all at the same time means that you'll be prepared to manage any project that is thrown your way, in any job you have.

11. Hold Your Own With Clients

Even at the most junior level, you will interact with clients, some of whom are high-level officers of companies or banks. Having direct contact with the general counsel of a public company is something not many people right out of school get to experience. Learning to hold your own among people in powerful positions means you'll be able to hold your own no matter where you find yourself next.

12. Develop Sound Judgment

Almost by osmosis, you will start to develop judgment. People will come to you for your sound advice and the ability to fix their issues. This is not just limited to your law firm life. Once you hone your skills and develop this somewhat amorphous "judgment," you will be able to use that skill in all aspects of your life.

13. Solve Problems

Problems, and therefore problem solving, come up daily in the life of a Biglaw associate. You're paid the big bucks to solve your client's issues, and to think outside of the box to fix them. Biglaw attorneys learn early on how important it is to be extremely resourceful. There is virtually no problem, big or small, that a Biglaw associate can't handle.

14. Develop a Keen Attention to Detail

There is no escaping the attention to detail you'll acquire in Biglaw. From day one, associates begin to develop this skill and it only grows as you spend more time in Biglaw. You'll likely never meet a Biglaw lawyer who doesn't obsess over the details of a transaction or a court filing and hold himself and his coworkers to the highest of standards. It is ingrained in Biglaw lawyers' heads like nobody else's to check and re-check things, to make sure not a detail is missed, and to always be on the look-out for possible issues.

15. Have Confidence in Yourself

Lastly, you will gain the confidence that if you can survive in a Biglaw emergency room – I mean, office – you can survive anywhere. You'll have the confidence to ask for what you want and to go for it, and the confidence to know that whatever task is set before you, you'll be able to tap into your Biglaw skills to conquer it.

~ ~ ~

While the work Biglaw firms do might at times seem esoteric and impossible to translate into a future career, when you take a step back, you'll realize that this is far from the truth. After just a short amount of time in Biglaw, you will have gained and mastered so many new skills that are transferrable to anything you choose to pursue in life.

Conclusion

What do I hope you got out of this book?

For those of you already in Biglaw, I hope, after reading this book and applying the skills highlighted throughout it to your own practice, that you will have become the go-to junior associate at your firm. I hope that you will have figured out how to work on the type of matters that you want, with the lawyers you want to work with, and on your own schedule (within reason). I hope you feel secure in your career because you've taken control over it and are directing it where you want to take it, as opposed to letting it take you along for the ride. I hope you have confidence in your abilities and feel like you belong in Biglaw, because if you got your foot in the door, you do belong, for as long as you want to be there. If you are struggling just to survive in Biglaw, I hope this book helped you reset the course. If you were stuck, I hope it helped you decide where to go next.

For those of you who haven't started your Biglaw job yet but hope to land one in the future, I hope this book helped to demystify some of the inner workings of Biglaw. That it pulled back the curtain, opened the kimono, and showed you things you otherwise only could have learned from working in Biglaw for many years. I hope that it gives you a head-start for when you begin your job and that you feel like you have the tools you need to succeed on day one.

For those of you who've already found success as Biglaw

associates before you picked up this book, I hope it helped you take your career to the next level. If the next level means partnership, I hope this book helps you get there. Now's the time where I hand you off to someone who can tell you all about what you need to do next to become a partner, and what it takes to succeed in Biglaw as a junior partner and beyond. If you follow the advice in this book, I'm sure you will be well on your way.

For all of you, I hope you find a career, whether it is in Biglaw or not, that fulfills you, that you choose not because you are "supposed" to, but because you want to, and that leaves plenty of time for whatever it is you decide to fill your unbillable time with. Thank you for reading and good luck in Biglaw and beyond!

Resources

The following resources have been instrumental in helping me navigate the ups and downs of my career, both during and after my time in Biglaw. They are the podcasts and books that I turn to again and again, and that I think all law students, Biglaw associates, non-Biglaw lawyers, and former lawyers can benefit from listening to and reading. Whether you are looking to up your game at work, are trying to figure out if you are in the right job after all, or need to feel like you aren't alone in Biglaw, I hope some of these resources resonate with you.

Podcasts Hosted by Lawyers

One of the easiest ways to add a little inspiration and guidance into your day is by listening to podcasts. Whether you listen on your commute to your Biglaw job or while running errands on the weekend, these podcasts will fill the time with great advice and open up your mind to all of the options that you have as a Biglaw lawyer.

1. *Hustle & Flow with Heather Hubbard.* Heather is a former Biglaw partner who now runs a successful business (including this podcast) helping lawyers find balance, happiness, and success in the law. Along with guest interviews, she talks a lot about goal setting and visioning (in a non-cheesy sort of way), and she gives practical tips on things like delegating and managing associates.

2. *The Happy Lawyer Project with Okeoma Moronu.* Okeoma is a happy lawyer and it comes across in every one of her

interviews, whether she is talking to another happy lawyer or a happy former-lawyer. (I am not sure whether Okeoma is currently putting out new episodes, but she has a whole library of great interviews that are available to download, so check those out and, hopefully, she picks the podcast back up!)

3. *The Resilient Lawyer with Jeena Cho.* If you are looking for a more reflective podcast or advice on how to de-stress and find more peace, Jeena's podcast is for you. Along with offering guided meditations, Jeena talks a lot about, and interviews guests on, calming the anxious brain and finding peace and happiness as a lawyer.

Productivity & Coaching Books

These three books have been the most useful to me when it comes to sticking to habits, boosting productivity, and becoming laser-focused on accomplishing what I set my mind to.

1. *Deep Work: Rules for Focused Success In a Distracted World*, by Cal Newport. This book is for anyone who is looking to regain their focus, a skill you need if you want to succeed in Biglaw. Maybe you used to be able to focus for long periods, but somewhere along the way you lost your ability to do "deep work." If so, this book gives practical tips that go beyond "put away your phone" that really work, if you implement them.

2. *The Alter Ego Effect: The Power of Secret Identities to Transform Your Life*, by Todd Herman. Perfect for the associate who struggles with imposter syndrome or feeling like he just doesn't fit in where he is in life. The author outlines a strategy for developing your own alter ego that you can bring to the table

whenever you need it, whether it's when you are giving a presentation to a client or motivating yourself to get to the gym to work out.

3. *Atomic Habits: An Easy & Proven Way to Build Good Habits & Break Bad Ones*, by James Clear. This book gives you the tools you need to transform your habits. By creating new systems in your life, you won't have to constantly force yourself to make decisions and start new habits. A key to success in Biglaw is managing your time, inside and outside of the office, and this book will help you put in place the systems to help you do just that.

Biglaw Novels

These novels were all written by former Biglaw attorneys, and the authors' familiarity with the Biglaw world shines through in each one. You might relate a little *too* much to some things the protagonists go through, but I had so much fun reading these and think you will, too.

4. *BIGLAW: A Novel*, by Lindsay Cameron. The story follows MacKenzie, a second-year associate in Biglaw who is struggling to have a life while working on the deal from hell with a partner from the same place. Beware: this one is so realistic it might trigger some flashbacks to your own, not-so-pleasant experiences in Biglaw.

5. *Love and Miss Communication*, by Elyssa Friedland. A senior associate at a high-profile Biglaw firm, protagonist Evie has devoted her life to her job. From the opening scene, where she tucks her blackberry into her underwear on her way to a wedding

(that she's late for, thanks to Biglaw), you can tell this book was written by a former Biglaw lawyer. This book is all about what can happen in life when you take a step back from the law.

6. *The Partner Track*, by Helen Wan. While this story follows another female associate protagonist, Ingrid, it is so much more than another novel about life in Biglaw. Outside of her fiction work, the author frequently writes about women (in particular women of color) and the challenges they face in the law. In this compelling novel, she weaves in stories about life as an "other" in Biglaw, the difficulties of trying to fit the mold when you weren't made for it, and the old-school culture of Biglaw that permeates many firms.

Books to Help You Find Your Purpose

Struggling to find what you are supposed to do with your life? You're certainly not alone. While I firmly believe that no one book has the answer to *that* question, these three books have given me the most clarity in my quest for figuring out what I want to be when I grow up. Whether you are happy in Biglaw or wondering if there is something else out there for you, one of these books might be the one to help you answer that question, "What am I supposed to do?" that almost all of us encounter at least once in our careers.

7. *Designing Your Life: How to Build a Well-Lived, Joyful Life*, by Bill Burnett & Dave Evans. This book will teach you that you don't just get the life you want, you have to *create* it. Written by two Stanford professors, the book shows you how to build the life you want by applying principles of design. If you like a book that includes plenty of experiments and practical tips, this one is for you.

8. *How to Live a Good Life: Soulful Stories, Surprising Science, and Practical Wisdom,* by Jonathan Fields. There are tons of books out there about how to live a happy life, but if you want to read one from the perspective of a former lawyer who "gets" lawyers and their particular struggles, this book is a great choice. The author shows you how to evaluate your life and make sure all of the "buckets" of your life are filled up. If you're neglecting one aspect of your life in favor of the others (something many lawyers tend to do), this book can help you rebalance the buckets. (The author has a podcast, too, by the same name, that is definitely worth checking out.)

9. *This Time I Dance! Creating the Work You Love*, by Tama J. Kieves. Hands-down, this book helped me the most when I was contemplating leaving the law. I suspect that everyone will react differently to the author's story about leaving Biglaw, but for me, it was a wake-up call. The author was asked by a friend, "If you are this successful doing something you *don't* like, imagine how successful you could be doing something you *do* like?" If that strikes a chord with you, definitely pick up this book for a little bit of "woo-woo" inspiration and a much-needed kick in the pants if you have been wanting to make a change in your life but haven't been able to do it.

The Unbillable Life: www.theunbillablelife.com

Lastly, I would be remiss to end this book without a mention of my own resource, my blog, The Unbillable Life (www.theunbillablelife.com), where the conversation about law firm life, success as a Biglaw associate, success after a Biglaw career, and more, is ever-evolving.

Check out the blog for posts about Biglaw associate life that didn't quite make it into the book, but that I think are equally as valuable for junior associates as what I've written about here. From how to survive late nights at the office (bring comfy clothes!) to tips about how to manage your finances as a Biglaw junior associate (don't get trapped by the golden handcuffs!), there are resources on the blog that I hope you will find helpful on your career journey.

Finally, if and when you are ready to leave the law, you can find even more information and resources for help with that on the site, too.

Reach out to me at: **marissa@theunbillablelife.com** with any questions or to share your story. I can't wait to hear from you and see where your J.D. takes you, to Biglaw and beyond! The possibilities are limitless!

Acknowledgments

Dad, for encouraging me since the beginning and for finding and correcting almost every unnecessary hyphen, typo, and mistake in this book (the remaining ones are my own), even if we will forever disagree on the use of the Oxford comma (it's my book, so I won the battle this time!).

Mom, for cheering me on, always, whether it was writing this book, starting a cookie business, or anything I've ever done in my life (even my failed attempts at drawing), and for setting an example for how to be a writer.

Guillermo, for believing that what I do now is a "real" job, for supporting me when I wasn't sure if I should tell my story on my blog, and for nudging my writing process along by periodically (kindly) asking me, "Sooooo, how's that book coming along?" when I would take months-long breaks from writing it.

And, finally, my Biglaw bosses, David and Charles, who displayed only kindness, mentorship, and encouragement throughout my whole time in Biglaw, and who taught me almost everything I've shared in this book (whether they realized it or not).

About the Author

Marissa Geannette graduated from the University of Southern California Gould School of Law in 2009 and spent eight years working as a Biglaw corporate associate in New York City. After leaving Biglaw, she started to write about her experiences there on what began as an anonymous blog called "The Unbillable Life" (www.theunbillablelife.com). Slowly, the blog morphed into a bigger, non-anonymous blog, where she continues to write about all things Biglaw and life after leaving it.

Realizing she had a lot to say about working in Biglaw, she decided to put her thoughts down on paper in a way that would be helpful to law students and new lawyers looking for tips on how to succeed in Biglaw. This book is the culmination of many years of hard work, both during her time at the firm (where she learned these skills and lessons) and after (when she finally sat down to put those experiences into words). Marissa lives in New York City, where she spends her days in comfy workout gear (whether or not she plans to go to the gym), happy that she no longer has a closet full of business casual clothes.

Made in the USA
Middletown, DE
27 July 2020

13625186R00149